Managing Quality in Health Care

Managing Quality in Health Care

P.R. Sodani

RAWAT PUBLICATIONS
Jaipur • New Delhi • Bangalore • Hyderabad • Guwahati

ISBN 81-316-0368-7

Published by
Prem Rawat for **Rawat Publications**
Satyam Apts, Sector 3, Jawahar Nagar, Jaipur 302 004 (India)
Phone: 0141 265 1748 / 7006 Fax: 0141 265 1748
E-mail: info@rawatbooks.com
Website: www.rawatbooks.com

New Delhi Office
4858/24, Ansari Road, Daryaganj, New Delhi 110 002
Phone: 011 2326 3290

Also at *Bangalore, Hyderabad* and *Guwahati*

Typeset by Rawat Computers, Jaipur
Printed at Chaman Enterprises, New Delhi

Contents

Preface

Improving quality of health care services is of critical importance for achieving the Millennium Development Goals in low- and middle-income countries, such as in India. Policymakers and decision-makers at district level thus need better understanding on planning, strategizing and implementing quality of care under the health system. By collecting and synthesizing what is known as the quality management of health services, this book fills an important void in our knowledge about how to improve quality of health services at district level for achieving the goals of National Rural Health Mission (NRHM) promoted by the Government of India.

This book has been developed as an introductory on managing quality in health care. It has been developed out of the teaching, training and research experiences of the author over two decades. The book will be of particular value to readers with interests in the areas of health systems, public health, health management, health policy and population policy. It has six chapters in all.

A major objective of the book is to synthesize literature on frameworks for quality of health care as discussed in Chapter 2, which would be helpful to not only the scholars working in public health but also managers who are involved in planning, designing and implementing quality of health care. Besides describing various framework for quality of health care, the chapter also provides working definitions of what is meant by quality in health care, with special reference to reproductive and child health services. Based on the primary sources, the author developed a framework for quality of safe motherhood and family planning services. In Chapter 3, the book describes how the quality of care is measured at the district level with respect to maternal and child health care services. Chapter 4 outlines the way to determine the factors that influence the current performance of quality of care at district level through systems diagnosis, which should be helpful for programme managers, researchers and policymakers.

In Chapter 5, the book delineates how strategies were developed by using the results from systems diagnosis to improve the quality of health care. Chapter 6 highlights important components of implementation of strategies formulated in the previous chapter to improve quality of health care. The messages emerging from this book are clear and hopeful: There are many ways to improve quality of health services. Measuring quality to assess the current level and using information to guide future decisions and inform stakeholders are important factors for successful implementation of quality of health care.

It is hoped that the book will be useful for those engaged in managing and researching quality in health care and performance management. Quality of care has been offered as a full course at the graduate and postgraduate courses on Health Management, Hospital Management, Hospital Administration, Public Health, and Health Systems and Policy. The book will also be useful to policymakers, project leaders, managers and scholars involved in planning, analysing strategizing, implementing, monitoring, controlling and evaluating quality in health care for improving the health systems performance.

Acknowledgements

The book is based on my research, teaching and training experiences at the Institute of Health Management Research (IIHMR), Jaipur, India. I would like to thank Shri M. L. Mehta, Trustee-Secretary, Dr Ashok Agarwal, Founder-Trustee and Dr S.D. Gupta, Director, IIHMR, Jaipur for their immense interest and encouragement for writing the book.

My interest in quality in health care started long ago when I was pursuing my Master of Public Health (MPH) and worked with my research supervisor Professor Sagar C. Jain at the University of North Carolina at Chapel Hill, USA. Subsequently, I carried out a number of studies in health systems for finalizing the Project Implementation Plan (PIP) for World Bank-assisted Rajasthan Health Systems Development Project at IIHMR, Jaipur, India. I would like to thank Dr S.D. Gupta, Director, IIHMR, Jaipur for providing me the opportunity to work with him on various important assignments, including research studies for strengthening health systems, designing and conducting training programmes at national and international levels, leading to improved knowledge on quality in health care. I would also like to thank Professor Udai Pareek, who passed away on 21st March, 2010, for his insight, motivation and helpful suggestions during our interactions at IIHMR, Jaipur.

I thank Rawat Publications for excellent publication of this book.

My wife, Rashmi, played an extremely crucial role in the completion of this book. Many a time she tolerated my absent-mindedness and created a warm atmosphere to complete this book. I also thank her.

P.R. Sodani

Abbreviations

ANC	Antenatal Care
ANM	Auxiliary Nurse Midwife
AO	Actual Output
AVSC	Association for Voluntary Surgical Contraception
BCG	Bacillus Calmette Guerin
BCG	Boston Consulting Group
CA	Competitive Advantage
CA	Cooperating Agencies
CHC	Community Health Centre
CMHO	Chief Medical and Health Officer
COPE	Client Oriented Provider Efficient Services
COPQ	Cost of Poor Quality
CPI	Client Provider Interaction
DHS	Demographic and Health Surveys
DMHS	Directorate of Medical and Health Services
DO	Desired Output
DPT	Diphtheria
DRS	Dual Rating System

EDD	Expected Date of Delivery
EFQM	European Foundation for Quality Management
EOP	End of Project
ES	Environmental Stability
FS	Financial Strength
FW	Family Welfare
GDP	Gross Domestic Product
GoI	Government of India
GoR	Government of Rajasthan
AIDS	Acquired Immunodeficiency Syndrome
HIV	Human Immunodeficiency Virus
ICOMP	International Council on Management of Population Programmes
ICPD	International Conference on Population and Development
IEC	Information Education Communication
IFA	Iron Folic Acid
IIHMR	Indian Institute of Health Management Research
IPPF	International Planned Parenthood Federation
IS	Industry Strength
IUD	Intra Urinal Device
LHV	Lady Health Visitor
MAQ	Maximizing Access and Quality
MCH	Maternal and Child Health
MCHO	Maternal and Child Health Officer
MIS	Management Information System
NHP	National Health Policy
NORAD	Norwegian Agency for Development

PAHO	Pan American Health Organization
PDSA	Plan Do Study Act
PHC	Primary Health Centre
PMP	Private Medical Practitioner
PRS	Performance Rating System
QA	Quality Assurance
QAG	Quality Assurance Group
QIQ	Quick Investigation of Quality
QOC	Quality of Care
RCH	Reproductive and Child Health
RH	Reproductive Health
SA	Situation Analysis
SAM	Service Availability Module
SC	Sub-Centre
SIHFW	State Institute of Health & Family Welfare
SPA	Service Provision Assessment
SPACE	Strategic Position and Action Evaluation
SRS	Sample Registration System
STD	Sexually Transmitted Disease
TOWS	Threats, Opportunities, Weakness and Strength
TT	Tetanus Toxoid
UNFPA	United Nations Population Fund
UNICEF	United Nations Children's Fund
USAID	United States Agency for International Development
WHO	World Health Organization
WHR	Western Hemisphere Region

List of Tables

List of Figures

CHAPTER 1

Introduction

Quality of care has emerged as the central issue in public health sector in India. The National Health Policy (NHP) of 1983 has set targets for improving the health status of the population and reducing fertility.

The Eighth Five-Year Plan (1992–97) document mentions the poor quality of the family welfare services offered by the programme as a major constraint that has inhibited the success of the programme. The approach paper to the Ninth Five-Year Plan in a review of the Eighth Five-Year Plan performance brings out that even though the Eighth Plan targets set for infant mortality rate and crude death rate are likely to be met, a significant reduction in the neonatal and maternal mortality is yet to be achieved. The Ninth Five-Year Plan is focussed on providing need-based, client-centred, demand-driven high quality integrated reproductive health services.

According to the National Health Policy (NHP) of 2002, the public health investment in the country over the years has been comparatively low, and as a percentage of gross domestic product (GDP) has declined from 1.3 per cent in 1990 to 0.9 per cent in 1999. The aggregate expenditure in the health sector is 5.2 per cent of the GDP. Out of this, about 17 per cent of the aggregate expenditure is public health spending, the balance being out-of-pocket expenditure. The central budgetary allocation for health over this period, as a percentage of the total Central Budget, has been stagnant at 1.3 per cent, while that in the states has declined from 7.0 per cent to 5.5 per cent. Given these statistics, it is no surprise that the reach and quality of public health services have been below the desirable standard (GoI, 2002).

Any expectation of a significant improvement in the quality of health services, and the consequential improved health status of the citizenry, would depend not only on increased financial and material inputs, but also on a more empathetic and committed attitude of the service providers, whether in the private or public sectors. In some measure, the NHP 2002 policy document is based on the understanding that the citizenry is increasingly demanding more by way of quality in health services, and the health delivery system, particularly in the public sector, is being pressed to respond. In this backdrop, it needs to be recognized that any policy in the social sector is critically dependent on the service providers treating their responsibility not as a commercial activity, but as a service, albeit a paid one. In the area of public health, an improved standard of governance is a prerequisite for the success of any health policy.

Recognizing the importance of health in the process of economic and social development and improving the quality of life of our citizens, the Government of India has launched the National Rural Health Mission to carry out necessary architectural correction in the basic health care delivery system. The goal of the Mission is to improve the availability of and access to quality health care by people, especially for those residing in rural areas, the poor, women and children (GoI, 2005).

Quality of care has emerged as a central issue in reproductive health. The need for improving quality is intensely realized, as the health services remain grossly underutilized despite an extensive network of infrastructure and manpower. The focus of the large projects at state or national level is mainly on infrastructure and manpower development, with less concerted attempts to improve the service utilization and service quality (UNFPA, 1992).

The above factors suggest that it is very important for Rajasthan to improve the quality of care in meeting the reproductive health needs of the community. The study, using a systems approach, identifies the causative factors and suggests a suitable strategy with a plan of action. The present study was carried out in Udaipur district of Rajasthan.

Justification of the Study

One of the fundamental requirements of quality is meeting the needs and expectations of the customer. Clients have certain needs and expectations, and the providers are required to learn about, investigate, understand, and implement methods for meeting them on a continual basis. Basically, it is a process of effective communication between the supplier or the provider of care or health service and the consumer or the receiver of that care and service. Improving the quality of care of health services is critical to improving women's health, increasing access to and use of reproductive health services, stemming the spread of AIDS/HIV and using scarce financial resources efficiently.

Quality of care is important for reproductive health programmes for two major reasons: (a) it enables clients to exercise their basic right and take decisions that meet their reproductive intentions. Hence, quality of care enables clients to order their own reproductive lives; and (b) it contributes to increased adoption and sustained use of the services.

One motivation for interest in quality of care issues is the fact that services are frequently underutilized. In addition to issues of cost, waiting time, and social obstacles, the critical reason for the underutilization of services is women perceiving the quality of care to be too poor to merit use (Parker et al., 1990). Another motivation stems from the fact that, while women are accepting methods of contraception, many are quickly discontinuing their use. Furthermore, clinic accessibility has not consistently shown a significant and uniform association with contraceptive behaviour either within or between countries (Mensch, 1992). Quality of care issues has also been shown to be a critical factor for prenatal care use (Parker et al., 1990; Locay et al., 1990; CIAES, 1991).

Quality of care also has an impact on where women seek care. It has been found in the Dominican Republic that women are willing to travel far to get to a clinic that provides better quality care; their motivation for going to a particular clinic is to get good and friendly treatment (Hardee and Gould, 1992). Studies in Latin America have shown that 50–70 per cent of emergency room cases are for primary care (Novaes, 1993). Instead of seeking treatment at the local primary care facilities, people travel to more distant hospitals because they perceive the quality of care to be superior. "Where potential patients have access to more than one facility, their judgment of the quality of care offered at these facilities often takes precedence over concerns about distance" (Thaddeus and Maine, 1990).

A key component of quality of care is the attitude of the providers. Clients are unlikely to visit a clinic where they have previously received degrading or dehumanizing treatment by providers. A study in Jamaica has identified poor attitudes of the providers as a major barrier to the use of prenatal care services (Wedderburn and Moore, 1990). In other studies, the "gender and attitude of health personnel emerge as important determinants of the utilization of maternal care" (Leslie and Gupta, 1989).

Programmes committed to providing high quality services best serve their clients with dignity and help them achieve their (health and) reproductive goals safely and effectively (Hardee and Gould, 1993). In addition, by serving the needs of clients, improved health status and contraceptive use can be attained more efficiently. A woman who receives a contraceptive method other than her first choice is more likely to interrupt her use of contraception (Pariani et al., 1991). Additional studies show that about half of the women who state they want no more children, but yet are not using contraception, are 'disenchanted former users' (Rogow, 1986). All of these studies indicate that more attention to quality of care will serve the clients' intentions, and will result in better reproductive health outcomes through more consistent use of contraception.

Quality of care is often considered unaffordable for programmes with scarce financial resources. Programmes lacking in quality, however, are extremely expensive because they waste human and physical resources (Simmons and Simmons, 1992). Women may use the health services, but because the quality of services is low, there may be no discernible result (Tinker et al., 1993). It is cost-effective to concentrate on a small number of annual acceptors and provide them with high quality services (Jain, 1988). More often, the critical bottleneck is not a lack of resources but poor commitment, values and attitudes. A review of small-scale diagnostic studies in family planning suggests that positive adjustments in any of the elements of quality of care have beneficial effects (Jain et al., 1992). Government policies that cut resources allocated to health services may save funds in the short-term, but will increase morbidity and mortality over the long term. Substantial improvement in quality of care is an investment, and may be the most cost-effective means of achieving better health outcomes.

In Rajasthan, Udaipur district is covered under tribal sub-plan area of the state. The district is characterized by rural, tribal, low socio-economic status and also low demographic and health status of the population. There is a high burden of reproductive health problems in the district, like unwanted pregnancies, unsafe abortion practices, and risky deliveries by untrained personnel, high incidence of reproductive tract infections/sexually transmitted diseases, and low awareness among adolescents about reproductive and sexual problems. The quality of reproductive health services provided by public health care system in Udaipur is very poor, and therefore, the clients approach traditional practitioners to receive services. Therefore, it is urgently needed to improve the quality of the reproductive health services in this area.

Objectives of the Study

This section includes objectives of the study, study area and definitions of key words used in the study. It also discusses methodology, data required, sources of data, methods of data collection, reliability of data, plan of analysis, and limitations of the study.

The present study has been carried out in the context of primary health care, with the following major objectives:

1. To assess the quality of care of reproductive health services.
2. To determine factors responsible for the current level of the quality of reproductive health services.
3. To suggest a suitable strategy to improve the quality of reproductive health services.
4. To suggest an appropriate plan of action to implement the suggested strategy for improving the quality of care of reproductive health services.

Study Area

The present study is focussed on improving the quality of care of reproductive health services in the context of primary health care. The reproductive health approach requires decentralized planning and implementation of services, so as to adapt to the diversity of reproductive health needs in different communities. Since continuous quality improvement calls for an interactive quality assessment, quality improvement cycle, health system managers should be allowed to plan as per local needs and resources. While it is necessary for all levels of the service system to be involved in the planning process, the optimal unit of planning has been identified at the district level. Rajasthan is a large state and unable to sufficiently attend to the specific requirements of sub-areas. Units smaller than the district has insufficient skilled manpower and resources to steer the planning process. Moreover, the devolution of administrative responsibility and authority to the district level makes it the appropriate unit also from the perspective of effective implementation of plans.

The study has been carried out for one district of Rajasthan, namely Udaipur. It has been selected for the study because:

1. The district is one of the 90 poor performing districts in India, identified by the Department of Family Welfare,

Ministry of Health and Family Welfare, Government of India. The poor performing districts are characterized by high birth rates, high infant mortality rates and very low levels of institutional deliveries.

2. The district, being one of the tribal districts of Rajasthan with about 40 per cent tribal population, represents the neglected districts in the state.
3. It is one of the districts in Rajasthan, identified by UNFPA for improving Health and Family Welfare services.

The present researcher is well aquatinted with the district and has had experience of working with the Health Department in various projects in the district. Hence, it was assumed that the district management would render better cooperation in collecting data and information

Key Terms

Quality of Care: In this study, we define quality in terms of the way individuals and clients are treated by the provider (Bruce, 1990). Using this principle, Bruce (1990) has evolved a working definition of quality of services that incorporates six elements: choice of methods, information given to users, technical competence, internal personal relations, follow-up or continuity mechanisms, and appropriate constellation of services. These elements reflect six aspects of services that clients experience as critical.

Choice of Methods: Choice of methods refers to both the number of contraceptive methods offered on a reliable basis and their intrinsic variability. Which are the methods offered to serve significant subgroups as defined by age, gender, contraceptive intention, lactation status, health profile, and, where cost is a factor – income groups? To what degree will these methods meet current or emerging needs (for example, the needs of the adolescents)? Are there satisfactory choices for those men and women who wish to space births, those who wish to limit them, those who cannot tolerate hormonal contraceptives, and so forth?

Information Given to Clients: Information given to clients refers to the information imparted during service contact that enables clients to choose and employ contraception with satisfaction and technical competence. It includes: information about the range of methods available and their scientifically documented contraindications, advantages and disadvantages; screening out unsafe choices for a specific client and providing details on how to use the method selected, its possible impacts on sexual practice and its potential side effects; and finally, an often neglected element, explicit information about what clients can expect from service providers regarding sustained advice, support, supply, and referral to other centres and related services, if needed.

Technical Competence: Technical competence involves, principally, factors, such as the competence of the clinical technique of providers, observance of protocols, and meticulous asepsis required to provide clinical methods such as IUDs and sterilization.

Interpersonal Relations: Interpersonal relations are the personal dimensions of service. Relations between providers and clients are strongly influenced by a programme's mission and ideology, management style, resource allocation, the ratio of workers to clients, and supervisory structure.

Mechanisms to Encourage Continuity: Mechanisms to encourage continuity can involve well-informed users managing continuity on their own or formal mechanisms within the programme. They can rely on community media or on specific follow-up mechanisms, such as forward appointments or home visits by workers.

Appropriate Constellation of Services: Appropriate constellation of services refers to situating family planning services so that they are convenient and acceptable to clients, responding to their natural health concepts and meeting pressing pre-existing health needs. Services can be appropriately delivered through a vertical infrastructure, or in the context of maternal and child health initiatives, post-partum services, comprehensive reproductive health services, or others (Bruce, 1990).

Reproductive Health: Reproductive health is a state of complete physical, mental and social well-being, and not merely the absence of disease or infirmity, in all matters relating to the reproductive system and to its functions and processes. Reproductive health, therefore, implies that people are able to have satisfying and safe sex life, and that they have the capability to reproduce and the freedom to decide if, when, and how often to do so.

Health Care Delivery System: Health care delivery system is a multitude of 'services' provided to individuals or communities by agents of the health services of professionals for the purpose of promoting, maintaining, monitoring, or restoring health. The health services are delivered by the health 'system', which constitutes the management sector and involves organizational matters.

Primary Health Care Level: Primary health care level is the first level of contact of individuals with the health system where primary health care is provided. The primary health care is provided by community health centres, primary health centres, and sub-centres.

Community Health Centre: According to Government of India norms, a community health centre is established in rural area for a 1,00,000 population. It is expected to provide specialist services and works as a referral hospital.

Primary Health Centre: A primary health centre is established in rural area for a 30,000 population in plain areas and a 20,000 population in tribal/hilly areas. It is staffed by a medical officer and other para-medical staff.

Sub-Centre: A sub-centre is established in rural area for a 5,000 population in plains areas and a 3,000 population in tribal/hilly areas. It is staffed by a health worker, usually an auxiliary nurse-midwife.

District: It is the principal unit of administration under a Collector. There are 32 districts in the state of Rajasthan. The districts vary widely in area and population.

Block: It is a unit of rural planning and development and comprises approximately 100 villages and about a 80,000 to 1,20,000 population, in-charge of a block development officer.

Panchayati Raj: It is a three-tier structure of rural local self-government, linking the village to the district. The Panchayati Raj bodies – Panchayat (village level), Panchayat

Samiti (block level) and Zila Parishad (district level) – are accepted as agencies of public welfare. All development programmes are channelled through these bodies. These institutions strengthen democracy at its roots, and ensure more effective and better participation of the people in the government.

Methodology and Approach

The present study is based on both primary and secondary sources. The study has used both quantitative and qualitative informations. The quantitative information has been collected from various published and unpublished sources. The qualitative information has been gathered through interviews with key personnel.

Figure 1.1

Stages of Managing Quality of Health Care

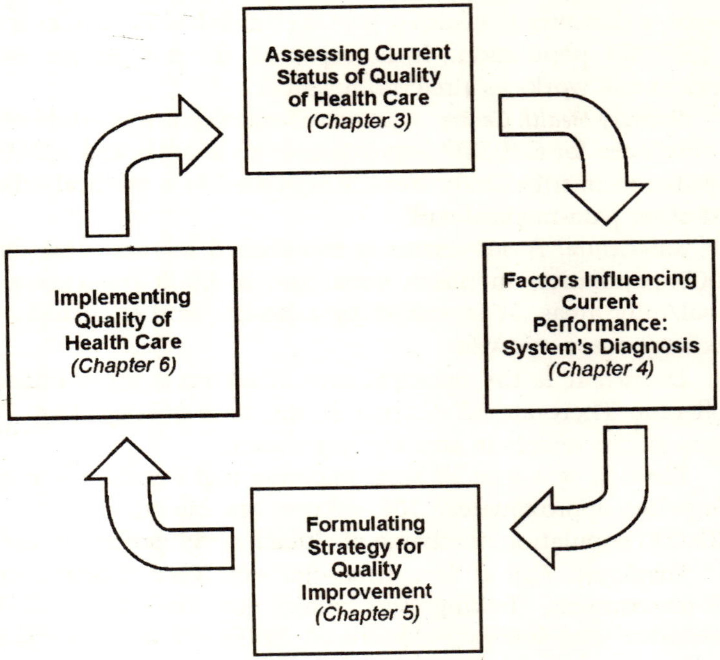

The following stages are used in the study for managing quality of health care in the study district (Figure 1.1):

Stage 1: Assessing current status of quality of health care.

Stage 2: Factors influencing the current performance: Systems diagnosis.

Stage 3: Formulating strategy for quality improvement.

Stage 4: Developing implementation plan for quality improvement.

Stage 1: Assessing Current Status of Quality of Health Care

In this study, to assess the quality of care in the study district, data generated by the Directorate of Medical, Health and Family Welfare Services, Government of Rajasthan, for Concurrent Evaluation of Reproductive and Child Health, Rajasthan (1997) were utilized. The concurrent evaluation was conducted during April-September, 1996 by the Government of Rajasthan to collect district specific baseline data on various aspects of quality of care.

In concurrent evaluation, sub-centre was the primary sampling unit and 30 sub-centres were selected in each district by adopting linear systematic sampling technique. From the selected sub-centre area, 30 currently married women, in the age group of 15–45, i.e., eligible women, were selected from the eligible couple register. The eligible couple register is prepared and maintained by auxiliary nurse midwives working at sub-centres. Among the 30 eligible women, five were currently pregnant; five had delivered during the previous two years; twelve were currently using some modern methods of family planning; three were those who themselves or their husbands had undergone sterilization; and five who were not using any method of contraception.

To assess the quality of care the Bruce Quality of Care Framework has been used. To measure the quality of care, it is necessary to make each element operational. The indicators identified to measure each element are provided in Table 1.1.

Table 1.1

Elements of Quality of Care and Indicators for Assessment of Current Performance of Quality of Health Care in the Study District

Elements of Quality of Care	*Indicators Used in the Study*
Choice of methods	Proportion of clients told about methods other than the one accepted at the time of adoption of family planning method.
Information given to clients	Proportion of clients told about side effects, risk, and both advantages and disadvantages, at the time of adoption of family planning method.
	Proportion of clients advised on periodic check-up during antenatal period, use of safe delivery kit (*Mamta* kit) in case of home delivery, and proper breast feeding to infants during postnatal period.
Technical competence	Proportion of clients inquired about general health problems and menstruation before providing family planning method.
	Proportion of clients for whom examinations were performed for blood pressure, vagina, and breast before providing family planning method.
	Proportion of clients for whom medical history was (obstetric history, general health, weight and height, expected date of delivery worked out, risk factors assessed) taken during antenatal period.
	Proportion of clients for whom examinations were performed for general physical health, obstetric problems and edema during antenatal period.
	Proportion of clients inquired about bleeding/pain in abdomen during antenatal period.
Interpersonal relations	Proportion of clients reported about home visit by health worker during previous three months.
	Proportion of clients satisfied with the assistance provided by the health worker during home visit.

Cont'd ...

Cont'd ...

Follow-up/continuity mechanisms	Proportion of clients told about precautions to be taken by the clients after adoption of family planning method for continuity.
	Proportion of clients received follow-up services after adoption of spacing method.
	Proportion of clients received follow-up services after adoption of sterilization.
	Proportion of clients received three visits at least during antenatal care.
	Proportion of clients received postnatal visit within a week.
Appropriate constellation of services	Operational indicator is not used.

The indicators listed in the table provide a detailed picture of the quality of services provided at the grassroots level. Each indicator is derived by using the frequency distribution for a single item, collected from concurrent evaluation. The raw frequencies are normalized by ensuring that all are measured on a scale from 0 to 100, where 100 is the highest score. The quantitative scores for each indicator are calculated in this manner. The summary scores for each element are the average of all the constituent indicators of that element, because each is felt to be of equal importance. Exactly the same considerations have been followed for the development of overall summary score of quality for the programme, each element weighted equally.

Stage 2: Factors Influencing the Current Performance: System's Diagnosis

Jain's Diagnostic Model (Jain, 1988) has been used to identify the factors influencing the current level of quality of health care in the study district. According to Jain's Diagnostic Model, the concrete way of describing a system is to say that its anatomy consists of five basic components, namely, desired output, environment, inputs, information, and process. Its physiology is characterized by the interdependence of these components, and change in one component vibrates through all the other components. The greater the degree of interdependence among components, the more cohesive is the system. The model is depicted in Figure 1.2.

Figure 1.2
Jain's Diagnostic Model: Factors Influencing Performance

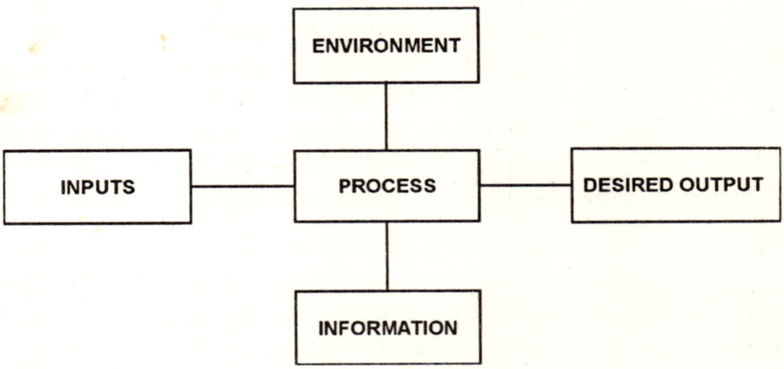

According to this model, a system's performance is a function of the *desired output, environment, inputs, information* and *process*:

System Performance = f(DO, Environment, Inputs, Information, Process)

The performance of the system is analysed by using the following equation:

Sp= AO/DO + (IO)

Where,

Sp = System Performance

DO = Desired Output

AO = Actual Output/Achieved Output

IO = Incidental Output

The ratio of *actual output* and *desired output* (AO/DO), which shows the level of actual output or achieved output in comparison to the desired output, measures the effectiveness of the system.

Desired Output

We have to find whether the system under study has any stated *desired output*; if yes, then, whether the *desired output* is measurable, acceptable by all the stakeholders, precise, and easy to understand.

Environment

Environment includes those factors, which influence the system, but are not under the direct control of the system processor. In other words, those are the 'givens'. A number of factors are identified as environment, influencing the quality of care in the district. Table 1.2 depicts the identified factors for the *environment* component of the system in the study.

Table 1.2

Factors Identified for Analysis of Environment Component of the System

Category	*Factors Identified*
Physical Characteristics	Geography and physical characteristics of the district
Socio-economic and Population Characteristics	Scattered population
	Female literacy
	Scheduled Tribe population
	Perception of community about health care
	Resistant community
Infrastructure Development	Transport development
	Communication development
Regulation	Regulation for private medical practitioners
Stakeholders	State government
	Donors' interest
	Research/training institutes
	Non-governmental organizations
	Traditional practitioners
Government Policy	State policy
Political Interference	Political interference in posting of doctors

The identified environmental factors are analysed and rated on a five-point scale in terms of their *importance* (how important the factor is in influencing the quality of care), *favourability* (the extent to which the factor makes a positive contribution), and *manipulability* (how easy it is to influence the factor).

Inputs

Inputs include all that enter the system on the consent of the processor. The consent may be automatic or imposed. The inputs mainly include resources (financial and manpower), technology (buildings and transport), customers, supplies, donations, etc. They are analysed in terms of quantity and quality. Table 1.3 depicts the identified factors in the study. The identified input factors are analysed and rated on a five-point scale in terms of their *importance* (how important the factor is in influencing the quality of care), *adequacy* (the extent to which the factor makes a positive contribution), and *manipulability* (how easy it is to influence the factor).

Table 1.3

Factors Identified for Analysis of Inputs Component of the System

Category	*Factors Identified*
Manpower	Number of doctors at community health centre
	Number of doctors at primary health centre
	Number of auxiliary nurse midwives at sub-centre
	Filled positions of doctors and auxiliary nurse midwives in tribal areas
	Manpower trained in interpersonal skills
Buildings	Number of health facilities
	Basic amenities at health facilities
	Location of buildings (health facilities) in the village
Supplies	Regular supply
	Distribution of supply
Equipment	Minimum necessary equipments
Finance	Maintenance of building/equipment
Clients	Clients defined and their use as input

Information

The quality (i.e., reliable, timely, accurate, complete, and relevant) information on all the other components (*desired output, environment, inputs and process*) of the system are needed by the manager for effective management of the system. The identified information factors are depicted in Table 1.4. They are analysed in terms of their *adequacy, quality, importance and manipulability*. The rating for each factor has been done on a five-point scale.

Table 1.4

Factors Identified for Analysis of Information Component of the System

Category	*Factors Identified*
Internal formal information	Service statistics reliability
	Eligible couple registers
Internal informal information	Personal experience, peers
External formal information	Concurrent evaluation
External informal information	Media, professional agencies, rumours

Process

It is the most important box. The *desired output* is achieved through process. The process has two components: (i) processor, and (ii) processing. The processor can be defined as the key players of the system who have the power/authority to achieve the *desired output*. The following characteristics, which influence the *processor* in *processing*, are measured in this study (3Cs): *concern* for quality of care, *competence* to provide quality services, and *continuity* with the system (Table 1.5). These are assessed for current status and manipulability on a five-point scale.

Processing is a function which achieves the *desired output* by manipulating all the components of the system. These are assessed on *importance, current status* and *manipulability* on a five-point scale. The processing is analysed on various management practices used in the system. These are manipulation of desired output (DO), manipulation of environment, manipulation of inputs, manipulation of information, manipulation of processor, soundness of strategy, implementing planning, monitoring, coordination and motivating (Table 1.5). These are assessed on current status and manipulability.

Table 1.5

Factors Identified for Analysis of Process Component of the System

Category	*Factors identified*
Processor	Concern for quality of care
	Competence to provide quality services
	Continuity with system
Processing	Manipulation of desired output (DO)
	Manipulation of environment
	Manipulation of inputs
	Manipulation of information
	Manipulation of processor
	Soundness of strategy
	Implementing planning
	Monitoring
	Co-ordination
	Motivation

Stage 3: Formulating Strategy for Quality Improvement

After careful diagnosis of the system, the strategy formulation is done through Jain's diagnostic model, portfolio analysis and strategic position and action evaluation (SPACE) analysis.

Stage 4: Implementing Quality of Health Care

A detailed plan of action has been developed for the formulated strategy, using resource matrix, implementation activity matrix, and activity scheduling.

Limitations of the Study

The study is based mainly on secondary data. It could focus only on family planning and safe motherhood components of reproductive health services due to lack of information. It had also to be conducted in a short period.

CHAPTER 2

Frameworks for Quality of Health Care

Recent attention to the quality of reproductive health services has highlighted the fact that, historically, these services have usually been evaluated more in terms of the degree to which they have achieved demographic objectives, such as fertility decline or the reduction of infant and maternal mortality, than in terms of the quality of the services deployed to achieve those outcomes. The quality of routine operations of reproductive health services that daily serve millions of people worldwide and that may have significant impacts on both safe and informed contraceptive choices and safe motherhood practices have become the focus of donor and government attention only in the last few years.

Although the issue of the quality of family planning services has been directly addressed only in the last few years (Bruce, 1983, 1990), various aspects of the programmes that are closely related to quality have been the object of research and discussion for a considerable time. The first studies concerned with quality characteristics of various reproductive health services focused on social, cultural, economic, and physical barriers to reproductive health services. These studies reported how shortcomings in the availability of contraceptive supplies and services, lack of information, problems of physical access, and psychological impediments acted as barriers to full utilization of existing services (Mundigo, 1973; Keller, 1973; Whelan, 1974; Mernissi, 1975; Scrimshaw, 1976; Pebley and Brackett, 1982; Lapham and Mauldin, 1985).

Recent discussions of family planning programme effectiveness have emphasized the importance of the interface of clients with the service delivery system, especially through their interactions with service providers (Simmons et al., 1985; Phillips et al., 1986; Lipton et al., 1987; Simmons and Lapham, 1987; Simmons and Phillips, 1990). Attention has shifted to understanding the dynamic nature of the process involved in accepting and adopting services. Providers are assumed to influence clients' contraceptive adoption and continuation through their skill, attitudes, and recommendations (Snowden, 1972; Rahman et al., 1990). Provider opinion has been shown to have a strong effect on client behaviour in some settings (Potter et al., 1987), and may also be an important determinant of contraceptive choice in family planning programmes especially those in which client-provider interactions are frequent, or where providers serve as promoters of national family planning policy.

Quality improvement in the provision of reproductive health services is expected to have an important impact on efficiency, client satisfaction and utilization (Geyndt, 1995; Satia, 1993; Pathfinder International, 1993). Quality of care is often considered unaffordable for programmes with limited financial resources. However, ensuring quality of care is more likely to result in a more efficient use of resources, because the interventions will have greater health benefits. It will result in a larger, more committed clientele of satisfied clients.

Donabedian's Framework

Donabedian (1980, 1988) emphasized a systems approach to health services, and provided a generic foundation for assessing the quality of health services, stressing that quality was a property of a programme involving all of the components:

1. Structure
2. Process
3. Outcome

Structure: Structure can be defined as comprehending the inputs to the services and the organization of those services. Structure includes human, material and organizational resources. This can improve the programme effort such as policy and political support; resources allocated, including staffing, equipment and infrastructure; and programme management and structure. In addition, the relevance of the service to meet the needs of the community/clientele and its accessibility may be considered under structure.

Process: Process includes the content of health care and the skill with which health care is executed. It includes the content, configuration and end points of the services, including prevention, diagnosis, information and therapeutic and rehabilitative services (Racoveanu and Johansen, 1995). Under content and configuration, Van der Waal et al. (1996) include elements such as:

- Information provided to the client
- Provider-client interpersonal interaction
- Choice (which may vary according to clients' conviction and desires)
- Efficacy of the treatment
- Effectiveness of the service in meeting its needs
- Technical skills
- Treatment (overall results and technical quality)
- Efficiency
- Provision of follow-up and continuity
- Workload
- Compliance with protocols
- Admission and discharge arrangements
- Range of services and referral facilities/process

Outcome: Outcome signifies what is accomplished for and by individual patients, patients as a group, or population as a whole. Most importantly, outcomes are improvements in health and well-being. Outcome refers to the end points and impact of the services provided. Impact in health had been defined to include:

- Client knowledge, satisfaction and acceptability of the treatment or service
- Change in current and future health status
- Prevention of morbidity, mortality and disability
- Quality of life
- Efficiency of resource utilization
- Use of services
- Continuation of treatment
- Equity and fairness of the service
- Community/family satisfaction (Donabedian, 1980)

Donabedian also stressed that in order to measure quality there needs to be first "concrete representations" or criteria and standards of structure, process and outcome variables. His work also contributed two important principles: the importance of the interpersonal dimension of care and the notion of client responsibility. Judith Bruce, having been informed by these two principles of Donabedian's model of care, developed the framework for assessing the quality of family planning services.

Bruce's Framework

Bruce's (1990) has taken the lead in trying to synthesize ideas and findings from previous research on barriers to contraceptive use, client-provider interactions and "user perspective" approaches to family planning. She has proposed that several programme features can be thought of as the operational components of quality of care in family planning programmes. These programme features are the six elements that together constitute quality of care:

1. Choice of Methods
2. Information Given to Clients
3. Technical Competence
4. Interpersonal Relations

5. Follow-up or Continuity Mechanisms
6. Appropriate Constellation of Services

These elements reflect *six aspects of services that clients experience as critical.* This framework is meant to provide an ordered point of departure from which to develop a description of the service unit and define its quality. The framework *is centred on the experience of those who have gained access to services.* The client usually does not see the apparatus behind her experience and all the vital work required to provide the services. Thus, the policies, resource allocation decisions, and management tasks that precede the delivery of services are not directly experienced, but their outcome, the service giving, is. As illustrated in Figure 2.1 the analytical framework proposed by Bruce (1990) links the hypothesized relationships between programme effort, quality of service experience, and its outcome. The six elements of the Bruce framework are described below (Bruce, 1990):

Figure 2.1

The Quality of Service Experience: Origins and Impacts

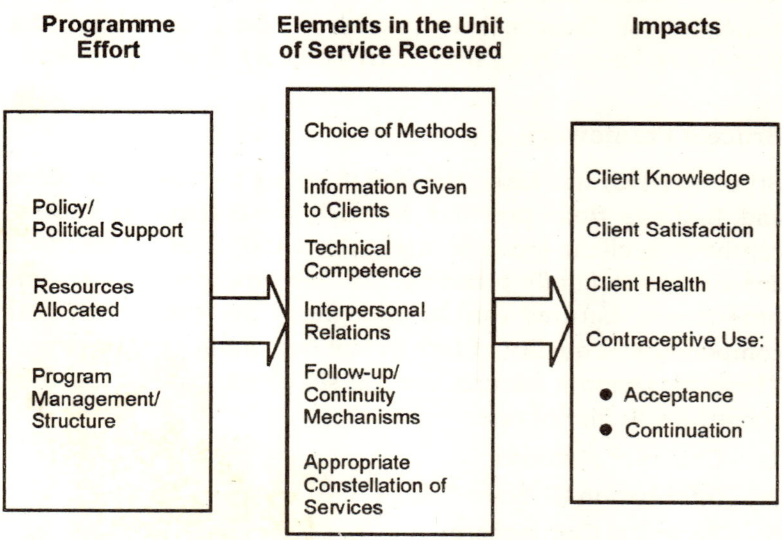

Source: Bruce, Judith (1990). Fundamental Elements of the Quality of Care: A Simple framework, *Studies in Family Planning*, 21 (2) Page 61–88.

Choice of Methods: It refers to both the number of contraceptive methods offered on a reliable basis and their intrinsic variability. Which are the methods offered to serve significant sub-groups as defined by age, gender, contraceptive intention, lactation status, health profile, and, where cost is a factor, income groups? To what degree will these methods meet current or emerging needs (for example, the needs of the adolescents)? Are there satisfactory choices for those men and women who wish to space births, those who wish to limit them, those who cannot tolerate hormonal contraceptives, and so forth?

Information Given to Clients: It refers to the information imparted during service contact that enables clients to choose and employ contraception with satisfaction and technical competence. Bruce says that it includes three aspects: first, information about the range of methods available, and their scientifically documented contra-indications, advantages, and disadvantages; second, close to counselling in the sense that provider and client seek a match from the safe methods for specific client, and finally, explicit information about what clients can expect from service providers regarding sustained advice, support, supply, and referral to other methods and related services, if needed.

Technical Competence: Technical competence is the element in the framework least easily judged by clients. It involves, principally, factors, such as the competence of the clinical technique of providers, the observance of protocols, and meticulous asepsis required to provide the clinical methods such as IUDs, implants and sterilization.

Interpersonal Relations: According to Bruce, the interpersonal relations are the personal dimensions of service. Relations between providers and clients are strongly influenced by a programme's mission and ideology, management style, resource allocation (for example patient flow in clinical settings), the ratio of workers to clients and supervisory structure.

Mechanisms to Encourage Continuity/Follow-up: Mechanisms to encourage continuity/follow-up can involve well-informed users managing continuity on their own, or formal mechanisms within the programme. They can rely upon community media, or on specific follow-up mechanisms, such as forward appointments, or home visits by workers.

Appropriate Constellation of Services: According to Bruce, the appropriate constellation of services refers to situating family planning services so that they are convenient and acceptable to clients, responding to their natural health concepts, and meeting pressing pre-existing health needs. Services can be appropriately delivered through a vertical infrastructure, or in the context of maternal and child health initiatives, post-partum services, comprehensive reproductive health services, employee health programmes or others.

The six elements of the Bruce framework are not utterly discrete. Their quality is interrelated often determined by common background factors and programme policies, operations management styles and resource limits. In addition to the six elements, however, the Bruce review provided a much broader conceptual basis for quality of care, which drew on earlier work on users' perspectives, on the work of Donabedian (1980, 1988) in health care, and on many studies of family planning care-giving process in developing countries. The work by Bruce and several follow-up articles stressed that this framework should not be used in any rigid manner, but according to programme need at the local level. The strength of the framework is the inherent attractiveness of the individual elements to programme managers and researchers. These six elements are interrelated. Further, the decisions regarding the intended and desired levels of care must be defined within the context of an individual programme by the key processors (Jain et al., 1992). Nevertheless, in the words of Simmons and Simmons (1992), the Bruce framework has "set the agenda".

Different Perspectives on the Bruce Framework

The Focus on Service-giving Process: The Bruce framework focused on the service-giving process (called 'process' by Donabedian) because the actual care given by providers and received by clients was a neglected factor in programme assessment. It suggested a focus on the *process* component of the programmes – the unit of service – though this is set in the context of *environment* and *input* variables (called *programme effort* variable by Bruce and *structure* by Donabedian)) which include policies, political support, resource allocation, programme management and structure variables, all important determinants of quality of care. For illustration purpose, a choice of methods is not possible without enough and regular supply of contraceptives. The interpersonal relations are strongly influenced by the quantity of care (i.e., frequency of client-provider interaction). The continuity of care provided is similarly influenced by access to supply points (i.e., service delivery points) and/or provider. Donabedian and Bruce place emphasis on technical as well as interpersonal dimensions of the care-giving process, and on outcomes for the client (client satisfaction, knowledge and contraceptive continuity). Measuring other aspects, such as policy and input factors, is important, but even where these are shown to be good, they cannot guarantee good process and outcome measures. The fact that technical care may be optimal but may not result in a satisfactory outcome is related in extreme form in the quip, "The operation was a success, but the patient died". More relevant examples are provided by Mensch (1993), where she describes what are in fact common situations: a programme with a good contraceptive logistics system which provides for a full range of methods, but in which providers give only biased information to women resulting in pushing certain methods; or clinics with staff who are technically well-trained but who treat clients poorly. The emphasis on process has been seen as both strength and a limitation of the framework. (Veney et al., 1993), writing from the standpoint of quality assessment, claim that not only does the focus on service delivery redress its previous neglect, but it allows quality to "stand independently of inputs to quality and outputs from quality", allowing evaluation of the interrelations among these aspects. On the other hand, Calla (1991) considers a focus on process as a limiting factor in quality improvement approaches because the process is so dependent on environment, especially input variables.

The Need to Include Access to Services as an Element: Some analysts have felt it crucial to add back the access or availability variable which Bruce acknowledged as important, but put it aside as something already receiving attention, in order to concentrate on the services actually being offered. Veney et al (1993) warn that addition to the Bruce framework of aspects such as resources available, management structure and capacity, and acceptability and availability of services draw us back to the Donabedian holistic view and detracts attention from the quality of the service delivery process itself. What was distinctive about Bruce's work—looking at the way the client was treated by the system—becomes diluted in the effort to capture the entire system.

More Emphasis on Outcomes: Loegering et al. (1994) assert that in the health care field both structure and processes of care-giving are over-emphasized compared to outcomes. Where outcome measurement is conducted, they claim it tends to be limited largely to short-term outcomes such as immediate response to treatment. The Bruce framework focuses on client knowledge, behaviour and satisfaction as the main outcomes, and suggests that these be viewed along a timeline with the long-term objective of meeting client fertility goals. In contrast to the health care field, long-term family planning outcomes or impacts, such as contraceptive prevalence and demographic impact in fact do receive high priority, whereas client outcomes, including short-term indicators, such as infections and other complications of methods, have been relatively neglected. Other client-centred outcomes such as client satisfaction are relatively new areas being explored in both health and family planning. There is a need for development of local standards for outcomes.

Client Defined Needs: Veney et al (1993) concur with the Bruce framework according to which any definition of quality must be multidimensional, but express the concern that the Bruce dimensions of quality care may not necessarily be the most appropriate, and that the key dimensions of quality may be perceived and defined differently by clients, by providers, and by donor agencies. The major criticism of this framework is that the elements have been defined by "experts" claiming to represent the clients' perspective, rather than by the clients themselves, and that this claim has not been validated empirically, a criticism highlighted during a USAID-supported seminar on management of quality (Hardee, 1994). The determination of client needs is a challenging exercise, which needs to be done locally and in context. Clients' views are difficult to obtain and/or tend to reflect very low expectation of care, both medically and in terms of interpersonal relations.

Adding Managers' and Providers' Perspectives: Debate on quality of care has also raised the issue of the need to determine the relevance of quality dimensions to different stakeholders, providers and managers in particular (Brown et al., 1993, Veney et al., 1993). The need to consider the role of managers and providers is acknowledged by Bruce as important in view of their determinant position in shaping the ultimate services, and also considering the low knowledge and expectations of clients. In a quality of care framework, however, it is vital for providers and managers to have a client orientation, to understand and focus the services based on clients' needs, and, to the extent possible, further develop clients' ability to demand improved quality of care. Providers as "internal clients" with needs of their own are also important.

It has been recognized that there is a potential conflict between the viewpoints of the major stakeholders. Providers may want to provide higher standards of care from a technical point of view, but have little empathy with the clients' ability to choose a method or their possible felt need for privacy in the care-giving process. Managers may give due importance to outcomes, which may have little importance for the provider. Moreover, managers tend to place greater emphasis on aggregate rather than individual outcomes. A basic question must be how far programmes can go in emphasizing providers', especially managers', technical, demographic, and related programme goals, and still adhere to the basic client-oriented principles of quality of care.

A regional workshop on quality of care held in 1992 yielded three definitions of quality of care from the client, provider and managerial perspectives, which show additional considerations added at each level:

- *Client Perspective:* Services that meet the needs of clients in achieving their reproductive goals.

- *Provider Perspective:* Services which meet the needs of clients, which are *medically safe and professionally ethical, and are accessible, affordable, and acceptable to women and men.*
- *Manager Perspective:* Services that meet the needs of clients and programme goals, which are safe, satisfying, affordable, accessible services, delivered in a technically competent manner *within the socio-cultural context of the country.*

IPPF Framework

Another widely used quality of care framework is developed by the International Planned Parenthood Federation (IPPF). The IPPF framework is "Clients' Rights and Providers' Needs" (Huezo and Diaz, 1993), which itself is multidimensional. The framework suggests that each family planning client has the following ten rights:

1. Information
2. Access
3. Choice
4. Safety
5. Privacy
6. Confidentiality
7. Dignity
8. Comfort
9. Continuity
10. Opinion

The ten needs of providers are:

1. Training
2. Infrastructure
3. Guidance
4. Respect
5. Feedback
6. Information
7. Supplies
8. Back-up
9. Encouragement
10. Self-expression

The IPPF framework has also been adapted by AVSC in preference to the Bruce framework, and the framework's dimensions form the basis for the revised COPE self-assessment checklist instrument (AVSC, 1994).

A fundamental principle of managing quality is that programmes must concentrate on the needs of both the women and men who use their services and those who might use their services in the future. These actual and potential users should be viewed as "customers": individuals with their own quality expectations, needs, and rights to decide for themselves whether or not to seek and use reproductive health services.

This customer orientation provides a new perspective for programme management as well: front-line providers are also seen as customers of the overall service delivery system. As *internal* customers, service providers require supportive management and supervision, readily available and appropriate supplies, and regular development and updating of skills.

The customer orientation is embodied in IPPF's Clients' Rights/Providers' Needs Framework, which addresses the needs of both internal and external customers. This framework is a basic reference document on managing quality in reproductive health and child survival programmes.

Professionals play a key role by developing technical definitions of quality. These definitions add technical specificity to clients' otherwise imprecise expectations of safety and efficacy, informed choice, and even privacy. The definitions must be codified and communicated through norms and standards, which must clearly state the quality expectations of individual workers and service sites.

In operational terms, quality means consistently delivering the services that best meet both client and professional expectations within prevailing resource constraints. Acceptance of resource constraints is essential. Even the poorest programme in the world can advance toward quality using its existing resources, as long as the programme ascertains, records, and communicates both its clients' needs and its professional standards.

The IPPF/Western Hemisphere Region (IPPF/WHR) further refines the definition of quality of care by considering the gender aspects of relationships between clients and providers. Gender refers to the roles, attitudes, values, and relationships affecting women and men throughout the world. The IPPF, in conjunction with three regional family planning associations and the Latin American and Caribbean Women's Health Network, has developed a manual for evaluating quality of care from a gender perspective, with an eye toward improving gender equity and sexual rights; assessing how well gender concepts have been incorporated into the institution; and strengthening staff members' ability to analyse how well they have integrated gender concepts into their delivery of reproductive health services.

The IPPF/WHR methodology, which has been tested in Colombia, the Dominican Republic, and Peru, indicates that while senior management and staff are generally committed to resolving gender and reproductive health issues, more work needs to be done to provide gender-sensitive services, such as counselling for women who have experienced gender-based violence, and to develop gender-supportive institutions, including antidiscrimination policies

The Rights of Clients

Information: Clients have a right to accurate, appropriate, understandable, and unambiguous information related to reproductive health and sexuality and to overall health. Information and materials for clients need to be available in all aspects of the health care facility.

Access to Services: Clients have a right to services that are affordable, are available at convenient times and places, are fully accessible with no physical barriers, and have no inappropriate eligibility requirements or social barriers, including discrimination based on sex, age, marital status, fertility, nationality or ethnicity, social class, religion, or sexual orientation.

Informed Choice: Clients have a right to make a voluntary, well considered decision that is based on options, information, and understanding. The informed choice process is a continuum that begins in the community, where people get information even before coming to a facility for services. It is the service provider's responsibility to either confirm an informed choice that a client has made or help the client reach an informed choice.

Safe Services: Clients have a right to safe services, which require skilled providers, attention to infection prevention, and appropriate and effective medical practices. Safe services also mean proper use of service delivery guidelines, quality-assurance mechanisms within the facility, counselling and instructions for clients, and recognition and management of complications related to medical and surgical procedures.

Privacy: Clients have a right to privacy during delivery of services. This includes privacy during counselling, discussions, physical examinations and clinical procedures.

Confidentiality: Clients have a right to confidentiality during delivery of services. This includes confidentiality in staff's handling of clients' medical records and other personal information.

Dignity: All clients have the right to be treated with dignity, courtesy, respect, consideration and attentiveness by the service providers during delivery of services.

Comfort: All clients have the right to be comfortable at the time of service provision. Service providers need to ensure that clients are as comfortable as possible during physical examination and clinical procedures.

Continuity of Care: All clients have a right to continuity of services, supplies, referrals and follow-up necessary to maintain their health.

Expression of Opinion: All clients have the right to express their opinions about the quality of services. Clients should be encouraged to express their views freely, even when their views differ from those of service providers.

Providers' Needs

Training: Health care staff needs knowledge, skills and ongoing training and professional development opportunities to remain up-to-date in their field and to continuously improve the quality of services they deliver. The providers need training on technical skills and communication skills for providing quality of health care services.

Infrastructure: Health care providers need appropriate material facilities and efficient organization reliable, enough inventories of supplies, instruments and working equipments and the infrastructure necessary to ensure uninterrupted delivery of high quality services.

Guidance: Health providers function best in a supportive work environment in which supervisors and managers encourage quality improvement and valued staff. Guidance from service guidelines, checklists, and supervision enables staff to perform their tasks well, and thus better meet the needs of their clients.

Respect: Health providers need respect and recognition from co-workers, managers, clients and the community for providing quality health care services. Efforts should be made in the health institutions to promote such organizational culture as to enhance the quality of care being provided by the providers.

Feedback: Health providers need feedback from managers, supervisors, co-workers and clients on the services being provided. This will help providers in improving the service quality. Efforts should be made in the health institutions to promote such practice as to enhance the quality of care being provided by the providers.

Information: Health providers need up-to-date information on technical issues involved in providing health care services to their clients. This will help the provider to continuously enhance the quality of services.

Supplies: Health providers need reliable, regular and adequate supplies of contraceptives, medicines, vaccines, equipment, and educational material necessary to ensure high quality of health care services to their clients.

Back-up: Health providers need back-up from other providers in the institution and also they need back-up for various levels of care for providing high quality health care services.

Encouragement: Health providers need encouragement form their managers and supervisors to recognize their good efforts timely and appropriate encouragement to provide good quality of health care.

Self-expression: Health providers need to express themselves to the managers and co-workers so that they can consider their views when making decisions. This will help providers to continuously enhance the quality of care. Efforts should be made to promote such behaviour in the health institutions.

PAHO Framework

The PAHO framework, developed for quality of care in women's reproductive health, for Latin America and the Caribbean, comprises nine elements. The framework is broadly based on Bruce framework (Bruce, 1990). This PAHO framework incorporates three delay's, namely, delay in deciding to seek health care, delay in reaching a health care facility, and delay in receiving health care at the facility. The nine elements of the PAHO framework are as follows:

1. Accessibility and Availability
2. Acceptability
3. Technical Competence
4. Essential Supplies, Equipment and Medication
5. Client Provider Interaction
6. Information and Counselling for Client
7. Choice of Methods (for family planning only)
8. Comprehensiveness of Care and Linkages to other Reproductive Health Services
9. Continuity of Care and Follow-up

The elements of the framework have been ordered to follow a woman's progression through the service delivery system. First, for example, she requires access to acceptable services. Then, she needs technically competent providers to give her the services. If client-provider interactions are unsatisfactory, it is unlikely that the information and counselling which the providers convey to the client will be heard and understood very well. This ordering does not imply that one element is more important than another; indeed some combination of all of the elements is necessary to provide quality of care to clients. Each element has corresponding indicators of quality, suggested methods for measuring quality, and recommended strategies for improving its particular aspect of quality.

Accessibility and Availability: Accessibility and availability are defined here mainly in the physical sense. The goal is not simply that services be available, but that the largest possible numbers of women are able to use those services. For health care services to be effective, women must know about the full range of services available to them and receive care at the lowest appropriate level of the system, i.e., at the primary level, if possible.

Acceptability: According to the framework acceptability refers to the cultural acceptability of services. Is there enough privacy? Can clients consult a female provider in situations where modesty would make that more desirable? Is confidentiality maintained? Are providers who are serving different ethnic groups sufficiently informed and sensitive to health customs and taboos?

Technical Competence: Quality of health care requires providers who are competent in clinical technique, and who adhere to standards and protocols for service provision, including meticulous asepsis. Competency-based training must be used to enable the providers to provide health care services and to ensure observance of standards and protocols. Adequate and constructive supervision is critical in providing health care services. Technical proficiency in providing safe and appropriate clinical treatment and knowledge of procedures for referring cases which cannot be adequately managed are essential to providing quality of health care.

Essential Supplies, Equipment and Medication: All health services need certain essential equipments, supplies and medication. For example, clinics and hospitals need gloves and sterile equipments to prevent the spread of infections. Norms and standards for necessary equipment at each level of care have to be established. Accreditation committees should be constituted based on technical criteria with representation from the public, private-for-profit and private-not-for-profit health sectors. In addition, quality health care means that the norms and standards for the availability of essential equipment, supplies and medication are met.

Client-Provider Interaction: According to the framework, the providers must treat clients with respect, be responsive to client needs and questions, be able to spend ample time with each client and avoid making moral judgements. Clients should be encouraged to take an active role in decision making.

Information and Counselling for Client: Again, clients must be given information on a range of health issues. Some of this information can be conveyed during group sessions with clients, but it is essential that each client have the opportunity to converse privately with a provider. In family planning, the provider must convey method options and use, contraindications and side-effects and the provider must seek to understand the clients' reproductive intentions and needs by obtaining information on their (a) background, (b) preferences, (c) contraceptive history, (d) reproductive intentions, and (e) health. In maternal health, it is essential that a woman (and whoever will be with her during labour and/or abortion) knows the danger signals indicating that she may go immediately to a basic emergency obstetric care or comprehensive emergency obstetric care. Women who have undergone an abortion need to be counselled about their rapid return to fertility and available contraceptive methods. Risk assessment, counselling and prevention education are vital for STDs/HIV services. Each woman must understand that copious vaginal discharge and/or pelvic pair are not just "her lot in life", but could be symptoms of serious medical problems which can be prevented or treated.

Choice of Methods: Further, in the context of family planning, women need to be provided with a choice of contraceptive methods based on their health profile, reproductive intentions, their risk for STDs/HIV, and preferences. Providers must also recognize the limits of most women's ability to negotiate contraceptive use and other aspects of sexual relationships. Informed consent, based on knowledge of options and consequences, is mandatory to achieve quality care.

Comprehensiveness of Care and Linkages Provided to other Reproductive Health Services: In the provision of contraceptives through family planning services, it has become increasingly evident that it is necessary to address other issues of women's reproductive health. By functionally segregating types of reproductive health services, the health care system of opportunities to make health services more effective, more efficient and more responsive to women's needs. With the advent of the AIDS pandemic, family planning clinics can no longer base contraceptive options merely on a client's reproductive intentions, but must also assess her exposure to sexually transmitted diseases and HIV.

Maternal health care is a unique opportunity to provide women with comprehensive reproductive health care, such as addressing their nutritional needs, their family planning needs, their post-partum or post-abortion family planning needs, prevention and management of physical violence and abuse, etc. The prioritization of these other health needs should be based on morbidity and mortality data complemented by focus groups discussions of women concerning their health problems. For example, in countries where cause of injury is not specified, or women are too scared to report physical abuse, this issue will not be reflected in epidemiologic data. But discussions with women's groups will pinpoint the importance of this issue. Since HIV/AIDS and STDs are so heavily stigmatized, particularly for women, it is critical that these services be integrated into other health services, such as family planning or maternal care.

Integration of reproductive health services does not necessarily imply that family planning, maternal health and STDs/HIV services should be provided jointly in the same location. In many local health systems it will be more appropriate for integration to occur on a smaller scale, through increasingly comprehensive information provided by counsellors or through a consistent and thorough referral system. Indicators in this framework help assess the extent to which these linkages are made through the services of the three components of women's reproductive health.

Continuity and Follow-up: According to the framework the last element is continuity and follow-up. The framework lays down that clients need to have continuity of care and appropriate follow-up of services. In family planning, women need to know when to revisit the care centre. In maternal health, women need antenatal care and post-partum care. For STDs and HIV, partner notification is an important part of continuity and follow-up.

ICOMP Framework

The ICOMP framework, which has three main dimensions: (a) user's perspectives; (b) service delivery perspective including provider's perspective; and (c) technology perspectives in an interface mode, which is, however, more comprehensive and relevant to reproductive health services.

1. User's Perspectives
2. Service Delivery Perspectives
3. Technology Perspectives

User's Perspectives: Different users have different expectations and may place differing emphasis on the quality of health care.

Service Delivery Perspective: Sometimes it is not the contraceptive technology but service delivery attributes – who delivers, how, where and when – that can make a difference in user's perceptions. For instance, it was found that the side effects of pills and IUDs did not differ between the experimental and control areas in an MCH-FP extension project in Bangladesh. But continuation rates in the experimental area were much higher because of better counselling. Quality can, therefore, be defined in terms of the process of service delivery and its capability to provide services at a desired level (Deming, 1982).

Service delivery can be improved in two ways: by changing the "common causes" that are systemic (and are thus shared by numerous service centres and providers) and removing the "special causes" that produce non-random variation within systems (and are usually confined to individual service centres and providers). Common causes would generally include poor design of services, inadequate or non-functioning equipments, poor training, poor physical conditions and so on. These are the responsibilities of management. Special causes would include lack of knowledge or skills of a particular provider or failure to follow the proper protocols for service delivery. The individual workers and their supervisors would be responsible for special causes.

The practical value of this distinction is enormous. Rather than placing the blame for poor quality on workers, it distinguishes the responsibility of workers and managers, thus reducing their frustrations. It also provides a mechanism for progressively improving quality of care. The current levels of quality using measurable attributes could be assessed and the extent of variation due to 'special causes' can be reduced by supervisors. While this would begin to improve average quality of care, management in collaboration with staff, should identify ways to increase system's capability to deliver services by addressing common causes.

In any service setting, the quality largely depends on the interaction between the service provider and client. Therefore, improving service delivery quality would have to focus on enabling, empowering and motivating providers to ensure a desired quality of care.

Technology Perspectives: Accepting user-based definition of quality in population programmes poses some difficulties. Users may not be able to assess the technical quality of services. Poor uneducated women may accept, or indeed even may desire, much less counselling on their choices than what may be considered desirable by knowledgeable health personnel. Instead they may wish to rely on provider's judgement of a method suitability for themselves.

Therefore, quality can be defined as "conformance to requirements" (Crosby, 1982). Any product or service that consistently performs according to its design specifications is of high quality. The goal of quality improvement is to have zero defects occurring. If management establishes a high standard of performance and renders it thoroughly to all levels in the programme then 'zero defects' is possible. This has been the approach for improving clinical practices for delivering higher quality of health care. A set of technical standards and necessary clinical practice protocols are set up. The quality is assessed by comparing actual practices with the standards and shortfalls are communicated to clinic managers. Based on this assessment, the clinic managers take necessary steps to improve the technical quality of health care.

UNFPA Reproductive Health Quality Framework

The UNFPA Reproductive Health Quality Framework comprises of nine elements. According to this framework, quality of care is defined as "attributes of a service programme that reflect adherence to professional standards, a congenial service environment and satisfaction on the part of the user." Each element has been defined and then described in more specific terms by "sub-elements", which have been given below in the form of queries or questions.

The nine elements have been categorized into generic and specific elements. Out of these nine elements, four have been grouped under specific elements, as they are particular to each reproductive health service while other five can be applied to any reproductive health services and therefore categorized as generic.

UNFPA Framework: Service Specific Elements

1. Access to Services
2. Equipment and Supplies
3. Professional Standards and Technical Competence
4. Continuity of Care

UNFPA Framework: Generic Elements

1. Service Environment
2. Client Provider Interaction
3. Information Decision Making
4. Integration of Services
5. Women's Participation in Management

Access to Services: Access to services is defined as "availability and accessibility of reproductive healthcare to clients, especially to underserved segments of the population (such as age, religion, men, women, old, young, among others) and marginalized groups (such as tribes, migrants, slum dwellers, among others)".

Sub-elements

- Are the availability of reproductive health services and their timings well marked on board?
- Are service providers available on a routine basis and in an emergency?

- Are these services affordable?
- What is the out of pocket expenditure for seeking reproductive health services? Expenses on medicines, diagnostic tests, providers fees, hospital charges, and opportunity cost (wages loss), travel expenses.

Equipment and Supplies: Quality of care in terms of equipment and supplies has been defined "in terms of functional status and quality of equipment and consumables supplied."

Sub-elements

- Are equipments of standard specifications available at the various health facilities?
- Are equipments functional and maintained regularly?
- Are adequate supply of drugs and contraceptives available?
- Is there a need-based procurement system and inventory control in place?
- Is the indent-delivery interval appropriate?
- Is the logistics management information system established and operational?

Professional Standards and Technical Competence: This is defined as the "availability of norms and service guidelines for procedure with administrative sanction for the same and provider competence for their observance."

Sub-elements

- Are service guidelines available at the healthcare facilities?
- Are providers' competences – clinical, communication and managerial skills – adequate for their prescribed roles?
- Are regular training courses organized for skill enhancement?

Continuity of Care: Continuity of care is defined as "continuity of services and records over a client's reproductive life cycle."

Sub-elements

- Is MIS stationery available and records well maintained?
- Is client follow-up regular and effective?

- Are providers able to manage or refer side-effects, complications, relapse or recurrence

Service Environment: It is defined as organization of services for the client's convenience and for maintaining standards. The Quality Assurance (QA) Checklists have questions that specifically address this aspect of quality.

Sub-elements

- Is there adequate physical space available in the health care institution(s)?
- Are there adequate specifications available for procedures in the health care institution(s)?
- Are water supply connection and adequate drinking water available as per the requirements?
- Are electric supply connection and regular supply of electricity available as per the requirements?
- Is adequate sheltered waiting area available?
- Is cleanliness maintained at the facility?
- Are clean toilets available separately for men and women?
- Is an adequate waste disposal system?
- Does the facility have provision for ensuring privacy and confidentiality?
- Are the waiting times for consultancy, tests and procedures reasonably short?
- Are policies and provisions in place for maintenance of facilities?
- Does regular maintenance of building and amenities take place?

Client-Provider Interaction: Client-provider interaction is defined as "the nature of provider-client relationship and information exchanged between them." The assessment of client-provider interaction cannot be directly observed in most cases as it violates the rights for privacy and confidentiality of the client. Also the presence of an observer will most likely alert the provider towards changing behaviour when observed.

Sub-elements

- Are providers courteous and respectful especially with vulnerable groups?
- Do providers actively listen to clients?
- Do providers give complete information and clear instructions to clients in simple language?
- Do providers use models, pictures, samples, pamphlets, posters and other communication aids while explaining to clients?

Informed Decision-Making: This is defined as "availability of relevant information and service procedures that facilitate informed choice by client."

Sub-elements

- Do the clients receive adequate and balanced counselling on methods and procedures involved in provision of services?
- Do communication efforts address social and economic determinants of health-related behaviour?
- Are client's decisions biased by incomplete information on available options, or by threat to deny some or all service(s)?
- Are those who switch or discontinue contraceptive methods encouraged to make another choice?
- Are there adequate procedures in place for informed consent before major clinical procedures?

Integration of Services: Integration of services is defined as "linkage of services and health institutions in order to provide comprehensive reproductive healthcare in a convenient manner."

Sub-elements

- What combination of reproductive health services is available at service delivery points?
- Are adequate upward referral systems across primary, secondary and tertiary institutions available? Are referred clients reverted to peripheral institutions after specialized care?

- Is there adequate linkage present between government, private, voluntary and corporate sector health institutions?
- Are referral protocols established?
- Is a system for coordinating interaction between different health sectors established?

Women's Participation in Management: This is defined as "accountability of a reproductive health programme to its clients, especially women by involving them in planning, implementation and monitoring of a reproductive health services."

Sub-elements

- What is the number and role of women managers and supervisors within the district healthcare system?
- Are there mechanisms for involvement of community/ panchayati raj institutions/women's group representatives in management of reproductive health programmes?

Relevance of the Bruce Framework for Safe Motherhood Programme

Since the Bruce quality of care framework for family planning services has been accepted worldwide, the present author has made an effort to see its relevance for other reproductive health components, say for *safe motherhood programme*.

Choice of Methods: It refers to both the number of contraceptive methods offered on a reliable basis and their intrinsic variability. Which methods are offered to serve significant sub-groups as defined by age, gender, contraceptive intention, lactation status, health profile, and, where cost is a factor, income groups? To what degree will these methods meet current or emerging needs (for example, the needs of the adolescents)? Are there satisfactory choices for those men and women who wish to space births, those who wish to limit them, those who cannot tolerate hormonal contraceptives, and so forth? Providing a choice does not necessarily mean that every programme must provide all family planning methods, but the overall programme effort on a geographic basis should be sufficient so that prospective users have reasonable, if not utterly equal, access to a variety of family planning methods.

Similarly, in *safe motherhood programme,* women should have reasonable access to various services required by a pregnant woman. The women pass through different stages during pregnancy, delivery and post-partum period, and therefore their needs and values change. The individuals pass through different stages in their reproductive life cycle, and their needs and values change. Pariani et al. (1987) found that whether a client's choice of method was "granted" or "denied" turned out to be more powerful than all other independent variables in explaining the tendency to continue or discontinue use of family planning services. It is necessary that clients decide, and the provider assists them in reaching a decision that is in their best interests. Clients should be in a position to decide the best possible course of action, based on their reproductive intentions, availability of services and ability to get the services. Informed decision-making leads to better outputs, and therefore may reduce maternal and infant mortality and morbidity. Informed consent, based on knowledge of options and consequences, is mandatory to achieve quality of care. The availability of health care commodities at a service delivery point is an obvious prerequisite for service delivery and for the choice of services that a provider can offer. Women who have had no antenatal examination are at risk as they may have an underlying complication or high risk. It is essential therefore that all women receive antenatal care and that their families make an informed choice about the place of delivery, i.e., institutional delivery or home based delivery, by a trained person or by an untrained person/relative based at the risk assessment of the pregnant women. However, the choice of method is less applicable to the *safe motherhood programme.*

Information Given to Clients: It refers to the information imparted during service contact that enables clients to choose and employ contraception with satisfaction and technical competence (Bruce, 1990). Bruce says that it includes three aspects: first, information about the range of methods available, and their scientifically documented contra-indications, advantages, and disadvantages; second, close to counselling in the sense that provider and client seek a match from the safe methods for specific client, and finally, explicit information about what clients can expect from service providers regarding sustained advice, support, supply, and referral to other methods and related services, if needed. It refers to the extent to which providers understand the needs of their clients and provide them information on contraceptive and safe motherhood practices that is accurate and comprehensible. It refers to what is said and done (content), rather than how it is said and done. For a family planning client to make an informed choice regarding a contraceptive method, the client should be fully cognizant of the potential side effects, risks, and advantages of the method offered. For a high-risk woman, to make an informed choice regarding where to deliver, she should be fully cognizant of the potential side effects, risk, advantages and disadvantages of the delivery place.

The clients' willingness to return to a service provider is also related in part to their comfort with client-provider interaction. Evidence (Haffey et al., 1984) indicates that most people remember messages better if the spoken word is reinforced by written or pictorial messages. Such visual materials support programme staff in remembering and systematizing all they are to transmit, and they help the clients as well. Research (Keller, 1973; Prabhavathi and Shenshadri, 1987) has demonstrated a strong relationship between the receipt of accurate information about methods, including anticipated side effects, and the propensity of clients to continue with the methods.

In case of *safe motherhood programme*, a client and her family members should be informed about the purpose of the antenatal care required for a pregnant woman. The provider should explain about early registration (within 12 weeks) of pregnant women at any service delivery point; at least three antenatal check-ups during pregnancy (the first at 20 weeks or as soon as the pregnancy is known and registered, the second at 32 weeks, and the third at 36 weeks) to monitor the progress of the pregnancy, and to identify and treat maternal complications early. The pregnant women should also be informed to visit more often, especially in the third trimester of pregnancy. It is necessary to explain to the client the increased requirements of iron and dangers of anaemia to pregnant women and therefore the need for her taking one tablet of iron and folic acid (large) daily for 100 days during pregnancy. The provider should explain to the pregnant woman that tetanus toxoid vaccination protects her and her newborn baby against tetanus which is a serious disease, which in most cases results in death. The National Family Health Survey, Rajasthan (1992–93) found that nearly two-thirds of the births were to women who did not feel it necessary to go for antenatal care, suggesting that they did not realize the importance of antenatal care for safe motherhood. This finding underlines the importance of the information given to clients to promote the use of antenatal care for safe motherhood.

Pregnant women and their family members should be advised that pregnant women need to take an extra meal every day; that alcohol and tobacco are prohibited for pregnant women; that a pregnant woman needs to rest on her side for about two hours in the afternoon, and get at least 8 hours of sleep at night; and that pregnant women must not do heavy work. It is important for the provider to advise the women and other family members so that family responsibilities are shared, and the pregnant woman gets the rest she needs. Clients should have the opportunity to talk to health care providers, and should be offered guidance on any health problems identified. Important elements of information include informing the community about early recognition of obstetric emergencies and the need for community efforts to arrange and finance transport to the health centre or hospital. Signs and symptoms of complications should be an integral part of the communication messages. Such messages should enhance the women's ability to use existing transport and to make appropriate decisions.

Pregnant women should be informed about safe and clean delivery: institutional delivery, and safe home delivery. In this part of the world, where a majority of the deliveries are still being conducted at home, use of *Mamta* kit (a safe delivery kit supplied free of charge by the state health department) for safe delivery at home should be recommended. The women who have delivered should also be informed about proper breast-feeding to the newborn and family planning services during the postnatal period. Women who have undergone an abortion need to be counselled about their rapid return to fertility and available contraceptive methods. Risk assessment, counselling and prevention education are vital for sexually transmitted diseases services.

Technical Competence: Technical competence is the element in the framework which is least easily judged by clients. It involves, principally, factors, such as the competence of the clinical technique of providers, the observance of protocols, and meticulous asepsis required to provide the service (Bruce, 1990). Technical competence refers to the skills, capability, and actual performance. Safe motherhood is a technical service requiring skilled providers. Quality of care is dependent on the training, experience, and skills of the providers, as well as protocols for asepsis, screening, clinical procedures, follow-up and emergency management. For example, to provide technically competent services, a village health worker must have the skills and knowledge (capability) to carry out specific tasks and to do so consistently and accurately (actual performance). Technical competence relates to how well providers execute practice guidelines and standards in terms of dependability, accuracy, reliability, and consistency. Providers who are uncertain in their skills are sometimes reluctant to use them or, worse, apply them badly. Neither approach contributes to the clients' reproductive health; rather, such performance generates negative rumours about the programmes and services. Competence-based training must be used to enable health workers, with or without medical degrees, to provide services and to ensure observance of standards and protocols. Adequate and supportive supervision is critical. Technical proficiency in providing safe and appropriate clinical treatment and knowledge of procedures for referring cases that cannot be adequately managed are essential to providing quality care.

Antenatal check-up involves careful recording of history and physical examination to determine whether pregnancy is progressing normally. The provider should also identify complications, which can adversely affect a woman's health or the health of the newborn. For noting case history, the provider should be competent in calculating the expected date of delivery, and assessing the risk factors. If the woman has any risk factor, the health worker should be competent to refer the woman at the right place at the right time to reduce any negative outcomes. The provider should also be technically competent to perform physical examination thoroughly, i.e., height, weight, blood pressure, abdominal examination, etc.

Interpersonal Relations: The "interpersonal relations" element in the framework has been separated from the information given to users because it is defined as the affective content of the client/provider transaction. It is this dimension, apart from the accuracy of the information given and the degree to which it is comprehended, that may strongly influence clients' confidence in their own choices and ability, satisfaction with the services, and probability of a return visit (Bruce, 1990). These are the personal dimensions of the service-giving process. Providers must treat clients with respect, be responsive to their needs and questions, and be able to spend ample time with each client and avoid judgmental attitudes. Clients should be encouraged to ask questions and to take an active role in decision-making. They should be encouraged to visit more often, especially in the third trimester of the pregnancy. This element broadly covers "how to communicate with the clients". It depends on the counselling and communication skills of the provider: building rapport, courtesy, empathy, active listening, respect for the client, etc. If a woman learns during pregnancy that she is infected with HIV, the first task of the provider is to offer her emotional support. Relations between providers and clients are strongly influenced by a programme's mission and ideology, management style, resource allocation, the ratio of workers to clients, and supervisory structure.

Mechanisms to Encourage Continuity/Follow-up: Mechanisms to encourage continuity/follow-up can involve well-informed users managing continuity on their own, or formal mechanisms within the programme (Bruce, 1990). A programme intended to establish continuity or follow-up mechanisms is one measure of its long-term commitment to individual welfare and a client-centred approach. Lapham and Simmons (1987) have argued that the test of quality of care lies not in its purely demographic consequences (i.e., couple productive rate, infant mortality rate, maternal mortality rate) but in the extent to which clients feel to have established a reliable relationship with a trusted provider and achieved a substantial measure of safe, effective, and comfortable control over their reproductive capacity. Jain (1989) has found that programmes can achieve better demographic results when they concentrate on a small number of annual acceptors and provide them with good care to enhance their satisfaction and thus improve the continuation rates than by trying to recruit a large number of acceptors at one time and not taking care of them. According to National Family Health Survey, Rajasthan (1992–93) percentage of institutional deliveries is higher among those who have had 4 or more antenatal visits (49%) than among those who have had 1–3 antenatal visits (22). This could be due to the availability of services for both antenatal and delivery care and/or to complications during pregnancy which may have led the women to seek more antenatal visits. It is also possible that increase in the number of visits could have established rapport between the provider and the user, which led the user to seek an institutional delivery. In the *safe motherhood programme,* the clients are crucially dependent on follow-up, resupply, and management of complications during pregnancy, and referral system in case of emergency. Incomplete antenatal care, unwanted pregnancies, early discontinuation of breastfeeding are all related to lack of continuing contacts between the client and the provider.

Though programmes may need additional resources to achieve the highest levels of continuation, more efficient use can be made of the existing clinic and field-worker time. Patient flow studies often identify means both to increase the clinic volume and to decrease client-waiting time (Hudgins and Merino, 1988). Supporting continuity of use among all clients may remain a desired goal, but priorities for specific follow-up must be set. For example, in the *safe motherhood programme,* a pregnant woman should get at least three antenatal care visits (the first at 20 weeks or as soon as the pregnancy is known and registered, the second at 32 weeks, and the third at 36 weeks). Women who have had no antenatal examination are at risk as they may have an underlying complication or high risk factor. Some women can even develop complications without any warning. It is essential, therefore, that all pregnant women receive antenatal care and advice on where to deliver. The postnatal period begins after the third stage of labour and includes the first six weeks after delivery. The suggested minimum number of contacts for providing postnatal care is four home visits followed by one clinic visit for each normal delivery conducted (Ministry of Health and Family Welfare, Government of India, 1996). The visits or contacts with the mother and her baby should be made within certain periods following delivery, so that specific health problems, which commonly occur during those periods, can be dealt with. More frequent visits are necessary if the mother or the baby has signs or symptoms of abnormal conditions. Maternal health care should be part of a continuum of care, comprising antenatal, delivery and post-partum care. Clients must, however, be seen as people with health needs that continue throughout their lives.

Appropriate Constellation of Services: Of all the elements in the framework, judgment about the adequacy of the "appropriate constellation of services" is the least universal, and most conditioned by context (Bruce, 1990). Only clients 'needs and managers' resources and imagination bound the possibilities. Given the possible variations, the evaluation of the appropriateness of the constellation of services is particularly value-laden. There are also several levels to this assessment. The most rudimentary level of judgment is whether the services are provided adequately within the articulated spectrum of the programme. A second level of judgment is whether the service constellation is appropriate to the needs of the client population. The appropriateness of the service constellation begins with an analysis of its competence. At the very least, any safe motherhood service should include a sufficient standard such that immediately related health screening that bears on the prescription of any service is available, so that they may be convenient and acceptable to clients, responding to their natural health concepts, and meeting pressing pre-existing health needs.

From the client's viewpoint, the different reproductive health services corresponding to stages in the life cycle should conveniently be available at the same or in linked institutions. There is a growing evidence that an appropriate constellation of services is necessary to improve the quality of any specific service. For instance, improving quality of care for intrauterine device (IUD) would require attention to diagnosing, treating and preventing reproductive tract infections. If such services are not available or the provider does not have the necessary competence for them, the quality of IUD services will be deficient. Similarly, in case of the *safe motherhood programme*, for example, improving quality of care for antenatal care would require attention to clinical assessment, physical examination, tetanus toxoid vaccination, and a steady supply of iron and folic acid tablets. If such services are not available or the provider does not have the necessary technical competence for them, then quality of antenatal care services would be deficient. In most settings, women see a close interrelation of their reproductive functions, and therefore, it seems perfectly reasonable to combine prenatal advice, delivery, post-partum services, and diagnosis and treatment of gynecological infections. Mothers also view their children's health as an extension of their reproductive well-being. For example, a recently delivered mother should be able to have a postnatal check-up for herself, immunization for her infant, advice on breastfeeding as well as contraceptive services, without having to make repeated visits for each service. Integration of services is also particularly important in catering to under-served groups such as adolescents. Maternal health care is a unique opportunity to provide women with comprehensive reproductive health care, addressing other issues, such as their nutritional needs, family planning needs, post-partum or post-abortion family planning needs, sexually transmitted diseases, etc. The prioritization of these other health needs should be based on morbidity and mortality data complemented by focus group discussions of women concerning their health problems. Diagnostic services for sexually transmitted diseases/HIV and pregnancy should be part of a comprehensive integrated programme.

Appropriate constellation of services would differ from setting to setting (Satia, 1994). For any programme, it generally includes convenient and acceptable complementary services to their users. For *safe motherhood programme,* it generally includes the complementary services like antenatal care, delivery, and postnatal care. Integration of reproductive health services does not necessarily imply that these services should be provided jointly in the same location. In many local health systems, it may be more appropriate for integration to occur on a smaller scale, through increasingly comprehensive information provided by counsellors or through a consistent and thorough referral system.

In summary, we may conclude that all the elements of the Bruce framework (except, choice of method) are relevant to the *safe motherhood programme*. Therefore, in the present study, we apply the Bruce framework to assess the quality of *family planning* and *safe motherhood* services.

CHAPTER 3

Assessing Current Status of Quality of Health Care

For measuring the quality of care, it is essential to make the elements of quality operational, first by identifying measurable indicators for each element, and second, by developing items to measure the specific indicators within each element (Mensch, 1994). In this respect, a sub-committee on quality of care of the Task Force Standardizing Family Planning Performance Indicators encouraged researchers to "let 100 flowers bloom", that is, to experiment with different approaches to evaluating quality with the expectation that promising methodologies would emerge from this broad experimental base (Helzner, 1990). A successor to the task force, the quality of care Sub-Committee of the Service Delivery Working Group, a group of primarily United States based professionals with experience in assessing quality, convened by the EVALUATION Project of the United States Agency for International Development (USAID), proposed a list of 42 core indicators of quality of care, based on the Bruce framework.

In the original framework, Bruce distinguishes conceptually between the "preparation" or readiness of the programme to offer quality services, the quality of service received by the client, and the outcomes of the service delivery process on client knowledge, behaviour, and satisfaction. Indicators of "preparedness" were developed to measure the managers' intentions and the providers' readiness to offer quality services. A second set of indicators was proposed to assess the quality of service received by the client during service delivery (Kumar et al., 1989). Others also stress the importance of distinguishing conceptually between the inputs (that is, the programme preparedness) and outcomes of service delivery, and the quality of the service delivery process itself (for example, Veney et al., 1993; Simmons and Elias, 1994).

Whereas a number of studies have used a variety of tools to measure some aspects of quality of care (Katz et al., 1993; Huezo and Diaz, 1993; and Simmons and Elias, 1994), relatively very few studies have attempted to measure all the elements of quality in a comprehensive manner. However, the types of data collection instruments used have largely determined which aspects of quality can be measured. The Situation Analysis methodology, developed by the Population Council (Fisher et al., 1992), has provided an important tool for the comprehensive measurement of quality of care. The combination of data collection instruments included in the situation analysis methodology has proved useful for identifying strengths and limitations of service infrastructures (including adequacy of contraceptive stocks, basic equipment for delivering clinical services, and recordkeeping mechanisms), the quality of services provided and received, and service delivery point performance.

Kaufman et al. (1992) provided an analysis of three aspects of service quality in four rural counties in China – the availability of contraceptive methods, information given to users, and provider knowledge about methods. The data were collected from a survey carried out during 1987. The survey was conducted in four counties located in Fujian and Heilongjiang provinces. A total of 318 married women of reproductive age were randomly selected and interviewed. The study reported that although providers believe they inform women about method choices and side effects, women were poorly informed about the methods they selected. Not all providers who insert

IUDs and distribute contraceptive pills were knowledgeable about contraindications and side effects of the methods.

Kim et al. (1992) evaluated the effect of a nurse training programme in family planning counselling skills on the quality of service delivery at the clinic level, as well as its impact on client compliance with pre-arranged appointments. The study used a quasi-experimental design to compare certified nurses who received six weeks of family planning technical training, with certified nurses who, in addition to the technical training course, received a three-day course in counselling skills. Data were collected through client exit interviews, expert observation, and inspection of medical record abstracts. Trained nurses performed better than their untrained counterparts in the quality of care areas investigated-interpersonal relations, information giving, counselling, and mechanisms for encouraging continuity. It was also found that the likelihood of clients attending follow-up visits was also found to improve when trained professionals attended them. The study revealed that short-term counselling training can significantly improve the quality of care provided by family planning workers, as well as client compliance with follow-up appointments.

Askew et al. (1994) presented the situation analysis approach as a means of collecting data that can be used to assess the quality of care provided by family planning service delivery points, and described the quality of services offered in Nigeria. The substantive results of the study suggest that although most of the 181 service delivery points sampled were functional, the quality of care being provided could be improved. Brown et al. (1995) conducted a study to heighten awareness of quality of care as a programmatic issue in the Moroccan governmental family planning programme and to test modified situation analysis instruments for measuring quality of care. Data were collected from 50 service delivery points in five provinces to measure six elements of quality in accordance with the Bruce framework. This study raises issues regarding the complexity of measuring quality, the ownership of results, and the appropriateness of a centralized study of quality in a decentralized programme.

Measuring Quality of Health Care in the District

To measure the current level of quality of health care in the study district of Udaipur, Bruce Quality of Care Framework (Bruce, 1990) has been used. According to the Bruce framework, quality of services incorporates six elements: choice of methods, information given to users, technical competence, internal personal relations, follow-up or continuity mechanisms, and appropriate constellation of services. These elements reflect six aspects of the services, identifying client experience as critical.

The data collected from the concurrent evaluation have been organized broadly in terms of the elements of the quality of care framework, and, within each element, according to a number of constituent indicators. The selection of indicators for each element is subjective, and has been determined by the nature of the data produced by the concurrent evaluation. The indicators for each element are given in Table 3.1. The indicators listed in the table provide a detailed picture of the quality of services provided at the grassroots level.

A procedure is proposed now for calculating a set of summary indicator scores that can be derived from individual indicators, with each summary score representing one element of the quality framework. Each indicator is derived by using the frequency distribution for a single item, collected from the concurrent evaluation. The raw frequencies are normalized by ensuring that all are measured on a scale from 0 to 100, where 100 is the highest score. The quantitative scores for each indicator are calculated in this manner. The summary score for each element is the average of all the constituent indicators of that element, because each is felt to be of equal importance. Exactly the same considerations have been followed for the development of the overall summary score of quality of health care for the programme, each element being weighted equally. This methodology has been used by Askew et al (1994).

Table 3.1

Quality of Health Care Indicators Scores for the Study District of Udaipur

Quality of Health Care Elements with Indicators	*Score*	*Sample size (N)*	*Description of Sample*
Choice of Methods	**57**		
Clients told about family planning method other than one accepted	57	(360)	Clients using spacing methods
Information Given to Clients	**25**		
Family Planning Services	4		
Clients told about side effects	5	(360)	Clients using spacing methods
Clients told about risks	2	(360)	Clients using spacing methods
Clients told about both advantage and disadvantage	4	(360)	Clients using spacing methods
Maternal Services	47		
Clients reported advice received on periodic check up	49	(300)	Clients receiving antenatal care and postnatal care
Clients reported advice received on use of *Mamta* kit	85	(300)	Clients receiving antenatal care and postnatal care
Clients reported advice received on breast feeding	8	(300)	Clients receiving antenatal care and postnatal care
Technical Competence	**30**		
Family Planning Services	25		
Clients inquired about health problems	36	(360)	Clients using spacing methods
Clients inquired about menstruation	22	(360)	Clients using spacing methods
Examination performed about blood pressure	21	(360)	Clients using spacing methods
Examination performed vaginal	22	(360)	Clients using spacing methods
Examination performed about breast	22	(360)	Clients using spacing methods

Cont'd ...

Cont'd ...

Maternal Services	36		
Medical history about obstetric history general	3	(300)	Clients receiving antenatal care and postnatal care
Medical history about health	5	(300)	Clients receiving antenatal care and postnatal care
Medical history about weight and height	42	(300)	Clients receiving antenatal care and postnatal care
Medical history about expected date of delivery (EDD) worked out	40	(300)	Clients receiving antenatal care and postnatal care
Medical history about risk factors assessed	40	(300)	Clients receiving antenatal care and postnatal care
Examination performed about general physical	57	(300)	Clients receiving antenatal care and postnatal care
Examination performed about obstetrics	8	(300)	Clients receiving antenatal care and postnatal care
Examination performed about edema	61	(300)	Clients receiving antenatal care and postnatal care
Inquired about bleeding/pain in abdomen	69	(300)	Clients receiving antenatal care and postnatal care
Interpersonal Relations	**45**		
Clients reported on provider's visit at home during last three months	74	(900)	All clients
Clients reported on satisfaction with services provides during home visit on reproductive health matters	17	(666)	Visited by health worker during last three months
Follow-up/Continuity	**27**		
Family Planning Services	36		
Clients told about regular follow-up	16	(360)	Clients using spacing methods
Clients told about reporting in case of side-effects	1	(360)	Clients using spacing methods

Cont'd ...

Cont'd ...

Clients received follow-up on spacing method	49	(360)	Clients using spacing methods
Clients received follow-up on sterilization	79	(90)	Clients using sterilization as family planning method
Maternal Services	19		
Clients received at least three visits during antenatal care	12	(300)	Clients receiving antenatal care and postnatal care
Clients received postnatal care visit within a week after delivery	27	(150)	Clients receiving postnatal care

The scores are presented here for two reasons. First, to illustrate that describing quality of care in quantitative, aggregate terms is possible. As the data in Table 3.1 demonstrate, clear difference exists between the elements scored, and this finding could be useful to managers in guiding programme development. A second reason for presenting them is the fact that these scores can be used by the programme manager to assess the services provided by their programmes. They are also helpful in developing a strategy for improving the quality of care. The scores cannot be said to represent good or bad quality, because absolute standards are inappropriate (Jain et al., 1992). They could be used, however, within a standard-setting process for the particular district, in this case, the study district. The scores could be used as benchmark to measure progress in improving the quality of services in the study district over the next few years. The following discussion describes each element of quality of care in detail with an analysis of the assessment of that element on the basis of some indicators.

Choice of Methods: This element of the quality framework is measured by one indicator, which indicates whether the provider presents an overview of all contraceptive methods to new users. Table 3.1 depicts that only 57 per cent of the clients in the study district were given an overview of all the contraceptive methods at the time of adopting the method. The concurrent evaluation (1997) revealed that for the state of Rajasthan as a whole, about 86 per cent of the clients were told about methods other than the one adopted at the time of the adoption of the family planning method.

This refers to both the number of contraceptive methods offered on a reliable basis and their intrinsic variability. Providing a choice does not necessarily mean that a programme must provide all methods; ideally a programme should offer a wide range of methods which are acceptable and accessible to all prospective users.

In other studies (for example, in a report from Indonesia by Pariani et al., 1991), evidence indicates that clients who receive their preferred method are more likely to continue using it than are clients whose choice, for whatever reason, is not granted. In this study, approximately half of the 91 clients who would have preferred another method received an IUD, 15 per cent received an injectable, and 14 per cent received the combined pill. An additional indicator of choice is referral for a method unavailable at the SDP on the day of the visit: Of the 28 cases where the selected method was unavailable, 14 were referred elsewhere. The Indonesian study clearly demonstrated that being able to exercise individual preference in the selection of a method also positively affects continuation.

Information Given to Clients: An important measure of the quality of family planning services is the provision of information to contraceptive users about method choices, efficacy, potential side effects of various methods, and what to do if problems occur. We asked family planning site managers and providers in the study about the approach, frequency, content, and thoroughness of information services. In order to measure the effectiveness of the information provided, we also asked clients what they knew about their chosen methods.

For a high-risk woman, to make an informed choice regarding where to deliver, she should be fully cognizant of the potential side-effects, risk, advantages and disadvantages of the delivery place. As Table 3.1 and Figure 3.1 indicate, a majority of the clients are not given any information on these aspects. Only five per cent of clients were told about possible side effects, two per cent were told about risks, and four per cent were told about both the advantages and disadvantage of the method. Table 3.1 and Figure 3.2 also show that only 49 per cent of the clients were advised on periodic check-ups, 85 per cent were advised on use of *Mamta* kit for safe delivery at home, and only eight per cent were advised on proper breast feeding.

Information has to be imparted during service contact that enables clients to choose and employ contraception with satisfaction and technical competence. This includes: information about the range of methods available, their scientifically documented contraindications, advantage and disadvantages; screening out unsafe choices for the specified client and providing details on how to use the method selected, its possible impact on sexual practice and its potential side effect; and finally, an often neglected element, explicit information about what clients can expect from service providers regarding sustained, advices, support, supply, and referral to other methods and related services, if needed.

Figure 3.1

Information Given to Clients for Family Planning Services

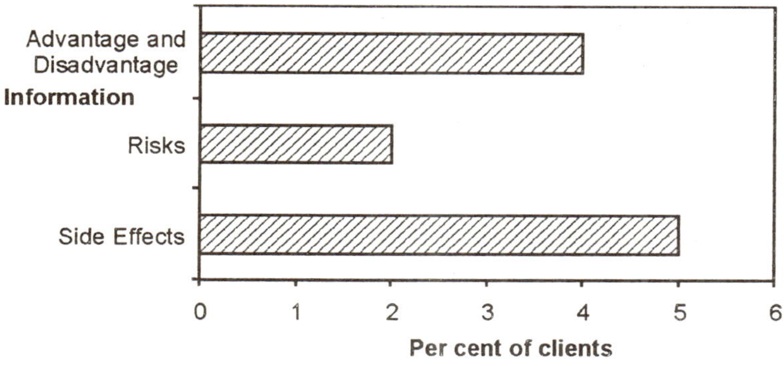

Technical Competence: In order to evaluate providers regarding their preparation for and competence in performing clinical tasks, we asked them about the content and duration of their medical training, including retraining, and the number of years of clinical experience they had. Information was also collected on supervision frequency and on the availability of a reference manual or checklist, especially when supervision was inadequate. Knowledge was evaluated by gauging the providers' ability to cite contraindications in using various contraceptive methods, to list common side effect of methods and clinical protocols for dealing with them, and to identify signs of serious side effects.

Figure 3.2

Information Given to Clients for Maternal Services

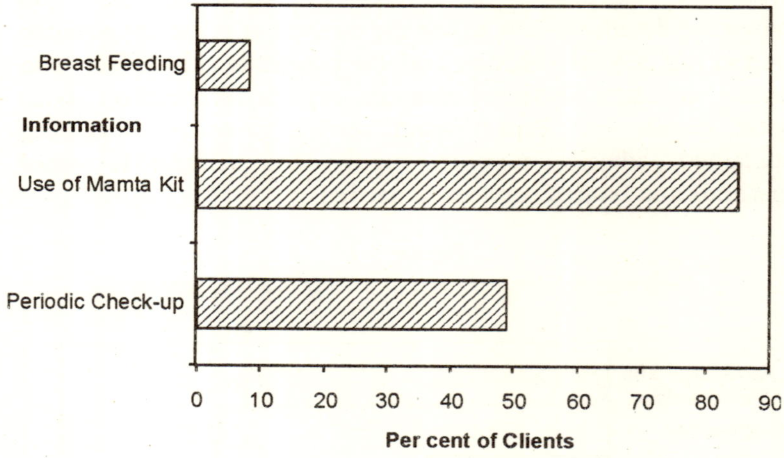

Technical competence is the element in the framework least easily judged by clients. Data used to judge provider competence in the present study is based on whether the provider offered services that are expected as a part of a competent service (as defined by an obstetrician/gynecologist, rather than by the actual quality of the services provided). In terms of measures of technical competence in case of family planning services, whether the provider enquired about the clients' health problems and menstruation status at the time of adoption, and whether the necessary examinations had been performed by the provider or not, are taken into account. Table 3.1 and Figure 3.3 show only 36 per cent of the clients were inquired about their general health problems and 22 per cent of the clients were inquired about their menstruation cycle, before providing the method. Moreover, 21 per cent clients reported that blood pressure was taken by the worker at the time of adopting family planning method, and 22 per cent reported that vaginal and breast examinations were performed by the health worker at the time of adopting the family planning method.

Figure 3.3

Technical Competence for Family Planning Services

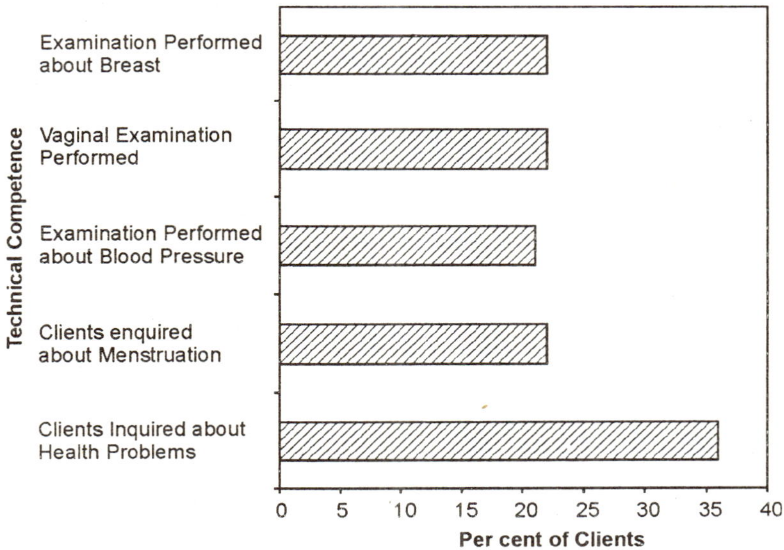

The technical competence of health workers in case of maternal health services is assessed on the various things the worker is expected to perform for a pregnant woman. These include: (i) taking medical history (obstetric history, general health, weight and height, calculating expected date of delivery, and assessing risk factors); (ii) examination (general physical, obstetric and edema) and (iii) inquiring about bleeding/pain in abdomen. Table 3.1 and Figure 3.4 indicate that only three per cent of women reported that obstetric history was taken, only five per cent reported that general health problems were inquired about, about 42 per cent reported that weight and height were recorded, about 40 per cent reported that expected date of delivery was worked out, and 40 per cent reported that risk factors were assessed for them in antenatal period.

Moreover, 57 per cent of the women reported general physical examination, eight per cent reported that obstetric examination, and 61 per cent reported that edema examination was performed for them by the health worker during antenatal period. About 69 per cent of the women reported that they were inquired about bleeding/pain in abdomen during antenatal period.

Figure 3.4

Technical Competence for Maternal Services

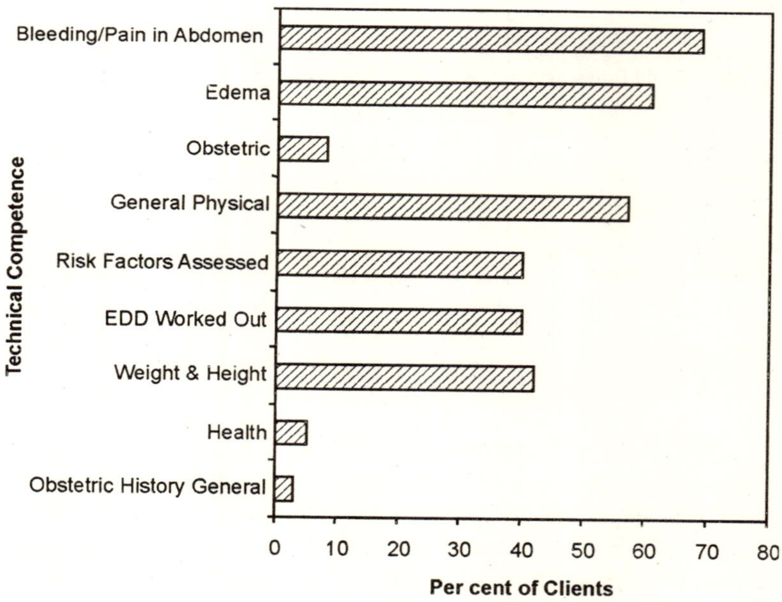

Interpersonal Relations: The "interpersonal relations" element in the framework has been separated from the information given to users because it is defined as the affective content of the client-provider transaction. In the present study, discussions with the district level officials revealed that each worker is expected to visit the client population at least once every three months. This makes for good rapport with the client. During the home visit, the worker is expected to provide assistance in home situation to the client. The situation is totally different from that of the sub-centre. In this situation, the worker is expected to maintain good relations with the client. The worker should devote a good amount of time, and approach the client in a pleasant and informal way to make the client feel easy and satisfied. Table 3.1 and Figure 3.5 show that about 74 per cent of the clients in the study district reported that the health worker had visited them at their homes during the previous three months. Out of those who had been visited by the health worker during the previous three months, only 17 per cent were satisfied with the assistance provided by the health worker.

Relations between providers and clients are strongly influenced by a programme's mission and ideology, management style, resource allocation (for example, patient flow in clinical settings), the ratio of workers to clients and supervisory structure. The objective of this factor is to measure the client-provider interaction in terms of client-worker contact and client satisfaction with service received.

Figure 3.5

Interpersonal Relations

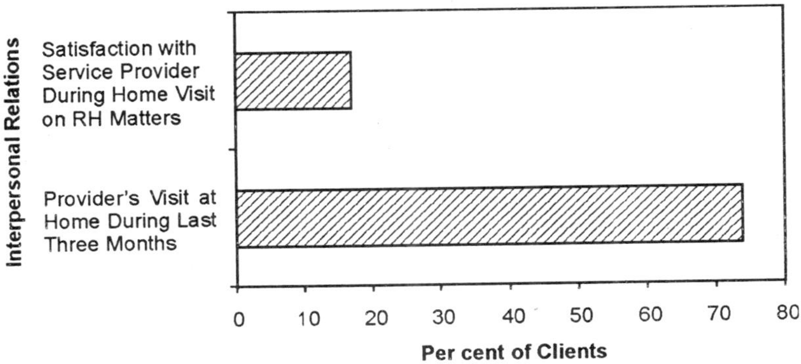

Mechanisms to Encourage Continuity/Follow-up: A service of good quality should enable a client to achieve her reproductive intentions; rather than emphasizing acceptance of a particular contraceptive method, a provider should encourage sustained use of family planning services for women seeking to space or limit births This element of service was measured by observing what the provider tells the client about follow-up and resupply and what mechanisms are available to facilitate follow-up. Although different contraceptive methods have different requirements for successful use, a provider can take certain actions to encourage sustained use (Robert et al., 1993), for a review of ways to reduce family planning discountinuation).

Mechanisms to encourage continuity/follow-up can involve well-informed users managing continuity on their own, or formal mechanisms within the programme. Table 3.1 shows that, in the district, only 16 per cent of the spacing method users were told about regular follow-up visit, and only one per cent of them were told about reporting to the health worker in case of side effects. Figure 3.6 shows that about 49 per cent of the current users of spacing methods received a follow-up visit by the provider within a month, and about 79 per cent of the sterilization clients received a follow-up visit after adoption of the method. In case of maternal health services, Figure 3.7 shows that only 12 per cent of the women had received at least three visits during their antenatal period, and about 27 per cent of women had received a follow-up visit by the health worker during the postnatal period within a week after delivery.

Figure 3.6

Follow-up/Continuity for Family Planning Services

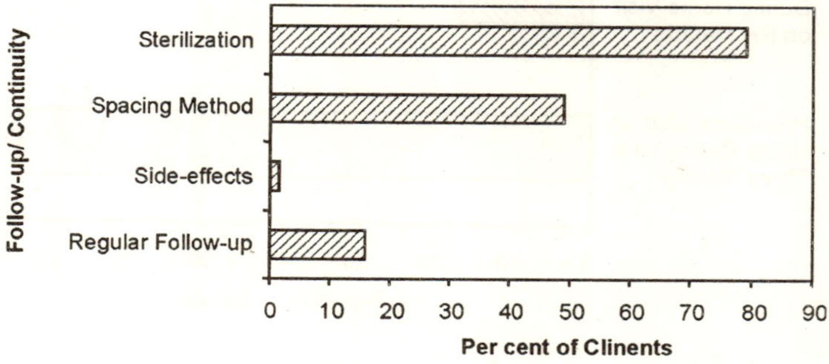

The programme involves well-informed users managing continuity on their own or formal mechanisms within the programme. They can rely upon community media or on specific follow-up mechanisms, such as forward appointments or home visits by workers. A mechanism to encourage continuity is quite essential for continuation of any method.

Figure 3.7

Follow-up/Continuity for Maternal Services

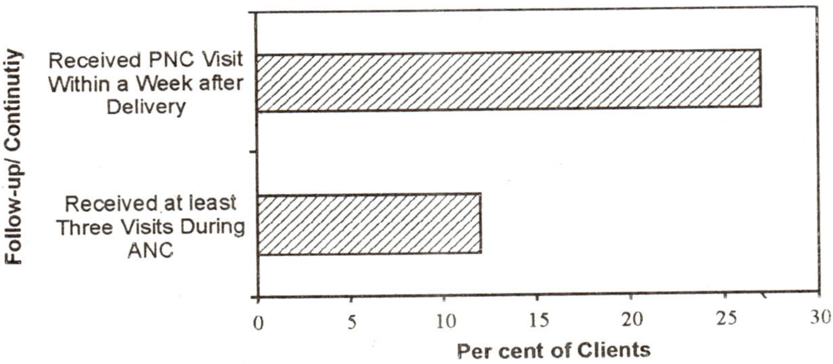

Appropriate Constellation of Services: It refers to situating family planning services so that they are convenient and acceptable to clients, responsive to their natural health concepts, and meeting pressing preexisting health needs. Services can be appropriately delivered through a vertical infrastructure or in the context of MCH initiatives, post-partum services, comprehensive reproductive health services, employee health programme and others.

Summary Indicator Scores

The data presented in this chapter have been organized broadly in terms of the elements of the Bruce framework. The summary indicator score for each element is given in Table 3.2. The overall score, based on the average of all the element scores, for the quality of care for the study district is 37. This shows that the current situation of quality of care in the district is poor.

Table 3.2

Summary Score on Elements of Quality of Care in the Study District

Elements of Quality of Care	*Score*
Choice of Methods	57
Information Given to Clients	25
Technical Competence	30
Interpersonal Relations	45
Follow-up/Mechanism for Continuity	27
Overall Score of Quality of Care	37

The reliability of these scores is based on the quality of data as well as sampling design of evaluation. There may be some sampling errors due to the smallness of sample size of particular groups of eligible women covered under the sample, and some non-sampling errors, to some extent, due to lack of a common training programme for the interviewers. Basically, the results obtained from the concurrent evaluation survey are reliable. In the next chapter, an effort will be made to identify the factors influencing for the current level of quality of health care in the study district.

CHAPTER 4

Factors Influencing Current Performance

In Chapter 3, an effort was made to assess the quality of care of reproductive health services in the district and it was observed that the overall quality of care score was 37 on a scale of 0 to 100.

In this chapter, an effort is to be made to determine the factors responsible for the current performance of quality of care in the district. To determine these factors, systems approach, employing Jain's Diagnostic Model has been used. The conceptual framework of Jain's Diagnostic Model consists of five components, viz., *desired output, environment, input, information,* and *process*.

Desired Output

In Jain's Diagnostic Model, the starting point is the desired output of the system. In the present study, 'system' is the quality of care of reproductive health services in the district. The system's performance, here, means performance of reproductive health services with respect to quality of care. It is observed that the system measures the performance of reproductive health services in terms of the number of clients receiving contraceptive methods (i.e., sterilization, IUD, oral pills and condom), and the number of pregnant women registered for antenatal services.

These performance indicators are not able to say anything about the quality of care being provided by the health department in the district. These performance indicators tell us about the coverage of the services only.

High performing systems tend to have a firm statement on the desired output. Further, this statement tends to be clear, precise, measurable, and acceptable to all major stakeholders. The Target-Free Approach is emphasized to provide quality services, but there is no guidelines and indicators for quality of care. An important finding of the study is that neither the Government of Rajasthan nor the Udaipur district authority provides a clear statement on the desired output pertaining to quality of services. What is stated is as follows:

> "The programme's performance should not be seen with respect to targets, but there is need to give more attention to the quality aspect" (GoR, 1996).

The quoted statement is just vague. It is not clear, precise, and measurable. The government had not set any specific indicators for measuring the quality of care. In the absence of a clear statement of goals, and sound indicators for measuring quality of care it is no surprise that so little progress has been made to achieve high quality.

Environment

'Environment' includes those factors, which influence the system, but are not under the direct control of the system processor. In other words, these are the 'givens'.

In providing quality of reproductive health services in the district, the environmental factors play an important role. The system has to depend on the physical characteristics of the area and the socio-economic and demographic characteristics of the population. The stakeholders, which include the Government of Rajasthan, non-governmental organizations, voluntary agencies, research and training institutions, private medical practitioners and traditional practitioners, have also influenced the system. Other factors, i.e., infrastructure development, policy guidelines, political interference and corruption have also influenced the system's performance.

Physical Characteristics

The study district of Udaipur is situated in the southern part of Rajasthan, and is oval in shape with a very narrow strip stretching towards the north. It lies between 23°46' and 26°2' north latitudes and 73° and 74°35', east longitudes. The district covers an area of 12,412 sq. km. The northern part of the district consists generally of an elevated plateau, while the eastern part has vast stretches of fertile plains. The southern part is covered with rocky hills and dense forests, whereas the western portion, known as the hilly tracts of Mewar, is composed of the Aravali range. Stretching from Bhim tehsil of Rajsamand district, the Aravali range runs south-westerly and spreads towards the valley of the Som river. There are two important passes in Aravali range, viz., Desuri Nal and Sadri. Udaipur district's major portion is covered with rocky hills, which have thick with forests. The river Banas and its tributaries flow through the eastern parts of the district. Other rivers in the district include Som, Jakham, Wakal, Sei, Sabarmati and Berach. All these are non-perennial rivers, which flow during the rainy season only.

These geographical conditions have resulted in vast rural areas with isolated communities and sparse distribution of households. It is responsible for lesser contact between service provider and client, which causes continuity in services to the rural and remote areas of the district. In the rainy season, some parts of the district get cut off from the district headquarters, because of rivers, affecting the supply of contraceptives and monitoring of district level officers.

Socio-economic Characteristics

The district is inhabited mainly (about 40%) by tribal people (Census, 1991). The status of women is very low. The uneven sex ratio might be explained by the unfavourable accessibility to modern health services for women. The literacy rate in the study area, especially among women, is significantly lower than the average literacy rate of the state. The broad stratum of literates in the district forms 35.5 per cent of the total population as ascertained during the 1991 census. However, there is still a marked difference in the literacy rates of the two sexes. Female literacy rate is falling behind male literacy rate in all parts of the district (in both rural and urban areas).

As far as the economic status of the district is concerned, the majority of the population is engaged in agriculture and agriculture related work. But, about 60 per cent of the workforce is unemployed. A majority of the population of the area belong to Scheduled Tribes (STs) (around 37%). This is a tribal belt, where most of the people are residents on hills and mountains. Hence, the nature of the population is not compact, but scattered.

The tribal people are very poor and backward, and their means of sustenance is either the forest products or the agriculture. The agricultural practices in the tribal areas are very primitive and they have to depend on the monsoon as the main source of water to irrigate their crops.

Marriage in Rajasthan is a ubiquitous phenomenon. Early adolescent marriage is common in the state, as well as in the district. According to the 1991 Sample Registration System (SRS) data, the mean age of female at effective marriage in Rajasthan is 18.3 years. In the rural areas, for girls below 18 years, the mean age is 15.9, and in urban areas, 16.1 years; the Indian figures being 16.0 and 15.9 respectively. According to concurrent evaluation (1996–97), about 27 per cent of marriages take place before 15 years of age, and 60 per cent of women are married by age 17 at state level, and the mean age at marriage for women in the state is about 15 years, which is much less than the legal age at marriage for women (i.e., 18 years) in India. In the study district, about 28.3 per cent of marriages take place before 15 years of age, and 54 per cent of women are married by 17 years.

Adolescent and child marriages have an adverse affect on the reproductive health of the mother and the health of the newborn. This, in turn, results in high maternal and child morbidity and mortality in the district. Early marriage has negative implications for both girls and boys. However, the consequences for girls can be more serious since marriage spells the end of education, premature assumption of domestic and child care responsibilities and severely restricted physical mobility. It is a well-documented fact that adolescence, a period of rapid growth, provides a second physiological opportunity for catch-up growth. However, a supportive environment is essential for maximization of this prospect. Pushing young girls into marriage robs them of this opportunity. Early marriage enlarges girls' fertility span, and malnourishment combined with early pregnancy results in physical wastage, birth complications and the delivery of underweight babies with a reduced chance of survival. While appropriate legislation to control early marriage exists in the form of the Child Marriage (Restraint) Act, 1978, its enforcement is a challenge in the face of social acceptance of this practice.

The community in the district is traditionally oriented and has little contact with modern society. Even today, a majority of the people have a traditional perception about diseases and their treatment. In case of illness, they often approach the local healers and other traditional health providers. It affects interpersonal relations of providers with clients.

Population Characteristics

The population of the district is predominantly rural in character. According to the 1991 census, about 82.9 per cent of the people live in rural areas. The district has recorded a growth rate of 22.5 per cent as compared to the state growth rate of 28.4 per cent. The growth rate in the rural areas of the district during the decade works out to 19.6 per cent, while it comes to 39.1 per cent in urban areas meaning thereby that the population of the district has grown at a faster rate in urban areas than in its rural areas.

According to the 1991 census, the density of population in the district is 167 persons per sq. km. There is a sharp variation in the density of population in rural and urban areas. In the rural areas, the density of population is only 161 persons per sq. km. The sparse population makes provision of reproductive health services by the health workers in rural areas very difficult.

According to the 1991 census, 8.3 per cent and 36.8 per cent people among the total population in the district belong to SCs and STs respectively. A majority among the SCs and STs reside in the rural areas of the district. Out of the total SC population, 78.2 per cent are rural based, and among the STs, 97 per cent live in the rural areas of the district. The situation influences the continuity of services.

Resistant Communities

The district health officials have identified the following communities as 'resistant' to accepting the family welfare and health services provided by the public health care delivery system: Banjara, Patel, Garasiya, Kalbeliya, Gadia Luhar and Kanzar. The Banjaras and Kalbeliyas are basically *nomads* who keep moving from place to place. Therefore, it is difficult for the district level health system to provide quality services to them in the matter of reproductive health. The other communities, due to their traditional beliefs and values, do not attach much importance to reproductive health services. It affects the interpersonal relations and continuity of services.

Infrastructural Development

The district lacks adequate infrastructure for transport and communication facilities. There is only one national highway, five state highways, and seven major district roads, which connect important marketing centres in the district. All the important places of the district are connected by bus routes. The district is connected by a metre gauge line of the Western Railway. A rail line, connecting Mavli Junction with Marwar Junction, passes through the district. A separate line joining Delhi, Jaipur and Chittorgarh with Udaipur passes through Mavli. The Udaipur-Himmatnagar line is also connected to Udaipur city. Transportation and communication infrastructure is available in towns and cities. In villages, the facilities of transportation and communication are not good as revealed in Table 4.1.

Table 4.1

Distribution of Villages according to Availability of Transport and Communication Facilities by Distance in the Study District

Distance	*Percentage of Villages Where the Facilities are Available*		
	Bus	*Railway*	*Telephone*
Within village	40.0	0.7	18.3
< 3 km.	26.2	5.6	29.9
3–5 km.	20.8	7.0	43.3
> 5 km.	12.9	86.6	8.3
Total (N)	100.0 (2,273)	100.0 (2,273)	100.0 (2,273)

Source: Office of Deputy CMHO (Family Welfare) (1997). *Integrated Family Welfare, MCH and IEC Plan, District Udaipur (1997–98).*

Accordingly, only 40 per cent of the villages have the facilities of bus transport, 0.7 per cent have the facility of railway transport, and 18.3 per cent have the facility of telephone in the village. Most of the community health centres and primary health centres will be adequately connected, if reliable and regular public/government transport is available. The road infrastructure to the more isolated villages and sub-centres is not adequate. Many hilly and tribal villages are connected by dust roads, making transport of referral patients from sub-centres or homes to referral institutions difficult. This influences the continuity of services in the district.

Stakeholders

There is a reciprocal relationship between an organization and certain other organizations, groups, and individuals. They are referred to as stakeholders, that is, organizations, groups, and individuals that have an interest or 'stake' in the success of the organization (Duncan et al., 1995). Some of these stakeholders are almost always powerful or influential, some others are influential regarding only certain issues, and still others have little influence and power. We identified the following stakeholders in this study: the Government of Rajasthan, donors, research and training institutes, non-governmental organizations/voluntary agencies, and traditional practitioners.

Government of Rajasthan: The Government of Rajasthan is keen to improve the quality of reproductive health services in the state. The Directorate of Medical and Health Services, Government of Rajasthan has initiated various efforts, i.e., conducting concurrent evaluation in the state for reproductive health services to improve the quality of services. The district officials would get full support for improving the quality of services from the state government.

Donors: Various international funding agencies are interested in providing funds to the district for the low socio-economic and health status of the district. The district is dominated by tribal populations. Therefore, a number of organizations are providing funds for the socio-economic development of the district. United Nations Population Fund (UNFPA), a major funding organization in Rajasthan, is working for improving the quality of care in reproductive health services. It has already taken the initiative to improve the quality of care in Bundi district of the state. In the past few years, many donors, i.e., UNFPA, NORAD, World Bank, and UNICEF, have provided funds for services related to reproductive health in the district. There are good chances for mobilizing funds for quality improvement in the district.

Research and Training Institutions: Various research and training institutions are working in the state, and they can be very supportive in improving the quality of care in reproductive health services. The Population Research Centre of Mohanlal Sukhadia University, Udaipur, located on the university campus in Udaipur, can be a good resource point for conducting surveys for client satisfaction and other aspects of the programme. The Population Research Centre is working on many other projects on the population programme in the state. Tribal Research Institute, a Government of Rajasthan organization in Udaipur, is working for the socio-economic development of the scheduled tribal population in the district, and is a good resource centre to know more about tribal culture and traditions. The Indian

Institute of Health Management Research (IIHMR), Jaipur, an organization dedicated to improving the health status of the people through training, research, and conducting consultations in health and health-related areas, offers a good opportunity for the system. The State Institute of Health and Family Welfare (SIHFW), an organization set up by the Government of Rajasthan, is also working in the field of training and capacity building of human resources in the health sector. It could be utilized by the system. The expertise available with these institutions could be manipulated for improving the quality of reproductive health services in the district.

Non-governmental Organizations and Voluntary Agencies: It is recognized by the Government of Rajasthan that non-governmental organizations (NGOs) and voluntary agencies have considerable advantage over the government system in terms of acceptance and co-operation with the local communities because of their personalized approach, high degree of motivation, sensitivity, and responsiveness to the peoples' needs. NGOs are flexible enough to experiment with innovative and alternative approaches in solving reproductive health problems.

There is a good number of NGOs and voluntary agencies in the district, mostly small ones. Most of the organizations are active in the area of agriculture and forestation, water supply, irrigation, and income-generating activities aimed at comprehensive socio-economic development at the community level, particularly among the tribal communities. In the reproductive health area, NGOs are less active in providing clinical services, but more active in awareness generating activities, providing information and education to the community on health-related issues. Some of the NGOs in the district, mainly the leading ones, receive support and funds for health and health-related activities directly from international organizations.

The major NGOs, namely, Seva Mandir and Astha are playing a pioneering role in the field of health care. Seva Mandir implements schemes, such as training of traditional birth attendants, provision of *Mamta* kits (safe delivery kits), provision of antenatal and postnatal services through traditional birth attendants at the community level. In addition, the organization aims at training pre-school teachers in first aid, hygiene, and sanitation. The agency is active in making awareness of sexually transmitted diseases and AIDS in the tribal areas, and areas close to National Highway 8, which passes through the district. The agency is active in supervision of workers by communities, and cost recovery of medicines, and has established local offices in the tribal areas. Astha, is a field based support/resource organization working with communities in the fields of capacity building, rural development and people's rights. The agency has a strong base in the district, and provides training to other non-governmental organizations and government personnel in the field of health-related issues.

Traditional Practitioners: The public sector and the private sector serve as complements to each other in providing reproductive health services in the district. Most of the traditional practitioners in the district are not registered. They are providing health care services through traditional systems of medicine.

In addition to the public health system and private practitioners of the allopathic system, a range of other unrecognized practitioners, known as traditional practitioners, play a leading role throughout the district, particularly in rural areas, because of the general reluctance to consult the public health system about reproductive and sex-related problems. Local traditional practitioners have an advantage over public health institutions. The traditional practitioners are likely to be part of the local community and known to the family members. Moreover, the traditional practitioners are likely to devote more time and attention to their patients than their allopathic counterparts. District officials reported that traditional practitioners may spend three or four times as much time with their patients as allopathic practitioners.

The role of the private sector is very important in providing quality care because most of the people utilise the services from the private sector, though the services being provided by traditional practitioners in the rural areas are of very low quality.

Government Policy

In 1992, the Ministry of Health and Family Welfare prepared an action plan for revamping the Family Planning Programme and recommended modification of the existing strategy of targets and incentives. The Sub-Committee on Population of the National Development Council (also known as Karunakaran Committee) also made similar recommendations. But, these recommendations could not be operationalized till 1995 when the Government of India started experimenting on a Target-Free Approach on a pilot basis in one or two districts in each state. The paradigm shift in the family welfare programme took place in 1996 when the Government of India adopted the Reproductive and Child Health (RCH) approach advocated at ICPD, Cairo, and introduced a Target-Free Approach all over the country. The Government of Rajasthan has also adopted the Target-Free Approach in its family welfare programme. Looking to the essential needs and recommendations of the Sub-Committee on Population, the Government of Rajasthan has introduced the innovative scheme of concurrent evaluation for the reproductive health programme in all districts as part of improving the quality of services.

Political Interference

Political interference occurs in several forms at various levels in the system. The more common forms are in purchase of medicines and equipment, postings and transfers, non-attendance at primary health centres and sub-centres, etc. It is difficult to gauge the exact extent of these problems and their impact on the system. But it is clear that, due to this, quality of service provision is made difficult for the system manager. Political interference in postings and transfers is routine and well known in the public health services in the district. It harms the overall authority and management of the system managers' effectiveness in improving the quality of services. There are several examples where strict and honest officers have been harassed in various ways by the subordinate staff with political support, and in such situations, the higher authorities do not support honest and strict officers. This has led to erosion of authority and accountability of officers and supervisors.

From the above discussion, it is clear that there are various environmental factors which contribute to the current level of the quality of care of reproductive health services in the district. But not all the factors are at the same level of *importance, favourability* and *manipulability*. Table 4.2 provides an analysis of these factors in terms of their *importance* (how important the factor is in influencing the quality of care), *favourability* (the extent to which the factor makes a positive contribution), and *manipulability* (how easy it is to influence the factor). The scoring of *importance* and *favourability* have been done on the basis of the findings of other researches reported in the literature, and the researcher's intuitive judgement, and of *manipulability* on the basis of discussions with the district level officials. The rating for each factor has been done on a five-point scale (1–5), where 1 denotes the lowest value and 5 denotes the highest value. A system of rating is used so that not more than 20 per cent items secure the same score. This is done to ensure greater degree of discrimination in scoring.

Table 4.2

Assessment of Environment

Factors	*Importance*	*Favourability*	*Manipulability*
Physical Characteristics	2	1	1
Socio-economic Status	2	3	2
Resistant Community	2	3	4
Tribal Population	1	1	2
Density of Population	1	1	1
Transport Development	3	3	2
Communication Development	3	4	3
Regulation for PMPs	4	2	5
State Government Support	5	5	3
Donors' Interest	1	4	3
Research/Training Institute	3	4	4
Role of NGOs/PMPs in Quality	4	2	5
State Policy/Guidelines for Quality	5	3	3
Political Interference	4	3	2

Inputs

Inputs are the things that enter the system on the consent of the processor. The consent may be automatic or imposed on the processor. The inputs mainly include resources (manpower, financial, etc.), technologies (building, transport, etc.), customers (pregnant women, mothers, family planning clients, etc.), supplies, donations, etc.

In this section, an effort will be made to analyse and assess the quantity and quality of inputs and their availability at the proper time in order to enable the system to provide quality reproductive health services.

To assess the adequacy of the available inputs and the extent to which they are in place, the extent of facilities and staff have been compared with the Government of India norms, wherever they existed. The gaps between the norms and sanctioned inputs and the inputs actually in place were compared. In cases where no government norms exist, interviews with facility managers were used to gauge their impression on adequacy of the inputs concerned.

Manpower

Health manpower can be divided into three categories: doctors, paramedical staff and administrative staff. There are certain established staffing norms for community health centres, primary health centres and sub-centres. The total number of staff in a district depends both on the extent to which facility norms have been met, and the adequacy of staffing of the existing facilities.

Table 4.3 shows that almost all the positions of auxiliary nurse midwives (ANMs) sanctioned at the sub-centre level are filled. The problem of vacant positions is slightly more in tribal areas, where about 2.8 per cent positions are lying vacant compared to the non-tribal areas, where only 1.7 per cent positions are lying vacant. Actually, the need for the availability of ANMs in tribal areas is more due to their being isolated tribal populations, and the community lacking easy access to health facilities.

Table 4.3

Availability of Auxiliary Nurse Midwifes at Sub-Centre Level in the Study District

Block	*Number of Sanctioned Posts*	*Number of Filled Posts*	*Number of Vacant Posts*	*% Vacant Posts*
Tribal Blocks				
Dhariawad	45	45	0	0.0
Gogunda	37	37	0	0.0
Jhadol	54	51	3	5.5
Kherwada	73	72	1	1.3
Kotra	42	36	6	14.2
Salumber	52	52	0	0.0
Sarada	54	54	0	0.0
Non-tribal Blocks				
Badgaon	22	22	0	0.0
Bhinder	53	52	1	1.8
Girwa	54	52	2	3.7
Mavli	42	42	0	0.0
Tribal Area	**357**	**347**	**10**	**2.8**
Non-tribal Area	**171**	**168**	**3**	**1.7**
Total	**528**	**515**	**13**	**2.4**

Source: Office records maintained at the Office of CMHO, Udaipur (as on August 1997).

Table 4.4

Availability of Medical Officers at Primary Health Centre Level in the Study District

Block	*Number of Sanctioned Posts*	*Number of Filled Posts*	*Number of Vacant Posts*	*% Vacant Posts*
Tribal Blocks				
Dhariawad	8	6	2	25.0
Gogunda	5	4	1	20.0

Cont'd ...

Cont'd ...

Jhadol	7	5	2	28.5
Kherwada	8	6	2	25.0
Kotra	6	4	2	33.3
Salumber	7	7	0	0.0
Sarada	9	8	1	11.1
Non-tribal Blocks				
Badgaon	3	3	0	0.0
Bhinder	6	5	1	16.6
Girwa	12	12	0	0.0
Mavli	9	9	0	0.0
Tribal Area	**50**	**40**	**10**	**20.0**
Non-tribal Area	**30**	**29**	**1**	**3.3**
Total	**80**	**69**	**11**	**13.7**

Source: Office records maintained at the Office of CMHO, Udaipur (as on August 1997).

Table 4.4 shows 13.7 per cent of the sanctioned posts of medical officers at the primary health centre level are lying vacant in the district. Comparison between tribal and non-tribal areas shows that the situation is more acute in tribal areas (where 20 per cent positions are lying vacant) than the non-tribal areas (where only 3.3 per cent positions are lying vacant).

It remains to be taken into account that medical officers do not want to work in tribal pockets due to lack of transport facilities and communication, non-availability of adequate housing, lack of good (English medium) schools for their children, and the feeling of isolation from the professional communities living in Udaipur city and nearby areas. Sometimes, fresh medical officers are appointed whose basic objective is not service, but to make preparation for examinations in higher education (most probably the post-graduate medical courses).

Table 4.5

Availability of Specialists at Community Health Centre Level in the Study District

Block	*Number of Sanctioned Post*	*Number of Filled Posts*	*Number of Vacant Posts*	*% Vacant Posts*
Tribal Blocks				
Dhariawad	9	3	6	66.6
Gogunda	6	6	0	0.0
Jhadol	10	7	3	30.0
Kherwada	9	7	2	22.2
Kotra	3	1	2	66.6
Salumber	9	9	0	0.0
Sarada	11	4	7	63.6
Non-tribal Blocks				
Badgaon	5	5	0	0.0
Bhinder	17	14	3	17.6
Girwa	6	4	2	33.3
Mavli	7	7	0	0.0
Tribal Area	**57**	**37**	**20**	**35.0**
Non-tribal Area	**35**	**30**	**5**	**14.2**
Total	**92**	**67**	**25**	**27.1**

Source: Office records maintained at the Office of CMHO, Udaipur (as on August 1997).

Table 4.5 shows that in the study district about 27 per cent sanctioned positions of doctors (junior specialists, senior medical officers and medical Officers) are lying vacant. This has resulted in acute shortage of doctors at the community health centre level (which includes positions of post partum centres, regional health and family welfare training centre, and block primary health centres, if working in the same building of the community health centre). The problem is more prominent in tribal areas, compared to non-tribal areas, where almost 35 per cent of the sanctioned positions are unfilled. The reasons are more or less the same as explained above for the medical officer at primary health centre level.

The above analysis was done with respect to the sanctioned positions only. We compared the sanctioned positions with the filled positions, and identified the gap between sanctioned and filled positions to know the extent of unfilled positions. The analysis suggests that there is less problem in case of posting of paramedical staff at the sub-centre level. The problem is more in the case of doctors at the primary health centre and community health centre levels in comparison to paramedical staff at the sub-centre level. Again, between primary health centre and community health centre levels the problem is more acute in community health centres. The tribal areas are suffering more due to unfilled positions affecting the quality of referral and other services

There are certain Government of India norms for staffing at the community health centre, primary health centre and sub-centre levels. As per the norms, at the community health centre level, 4 doctors should be available. But, in Udaipur, on an average, sanctioned positions of doctors are 5.4 and filled positions are 3.9 (which include positions of post partum centres, regional health and family welfare training centre, and block primary health centres, if working in the same building of the community health centre) at the community health centre level. At primary health centre level, as per Government of India norms, 2 doctors, 7 paramedical, and 7 administrative staff should be available, but in case of the district, on an average, 1.1 doctors, 4.2 paramedical and 2.9 administrative staff are sanctioned and only 0.95 doctors, 2.8 paramedical and 2.5 administrative staff are actually filled. At the sub-centre level, two paramedicals (male and female) should be available as per the norms, but only one post (female multipurpose worker) is sanctioned and 0.97 filled. This analysis shows that there exists a serious problem in the availability of staff as per norms set by the Government of India. The analysis shows also that there is an acute shortage of medical officers at the community health centre and primary health centre levels, particularly in tribal areas where about 37 per cent of the population reside.

It has resulted in inadequate and non-functioning of an effective referral system in the district and causes a lowering in the quality of care when needed. Therefore, the ANM is also not confident in referring the patients at community health centre level in case of emergencies. This shows that there is a high turnover of physicians in rural areas. They are not interested in taking the government positions because of low salary structure, and lack of regular update of professional knowledge and skills, lack of adequate diagnostic facilities, and lack of adequate accommodation and schooling for their children. In addition to this, there are problems of staff shortage, absenteeism (authorized and unauthorized), and perpetual personnel transfers. These factors influence the quality of care by affecting the low continuity of care, and weaken interpersonal relations between clients and providers.

Building of Health Facilities

There are facility norms required to serve the rural population. The Bhore committee set down certain norms that were pursued in the initial five-year plans. During the Sixth Plan (1980–85), new norms were laid down for population coverage and staffing of community health centres, primary health centres and sub-centres. These were one community health centre per 1,00,000 population, one primary health centre per 30,000 population (20,000 in hilly, tribal and backward areas), and one sub-centre per 5,000 population (3,000 in hilly, tribal and backward areas). In the district, out of the total 11 blocks, seven are in hill and tribal areas and the remaining four in the plains.

Table 4.6

Availability of Health Care Institutions in the Study District

Block	*Number of CHCs Functioning*	*Number of PHCs Functioning*	*Number of Sub-centres Functioning*
Tribal Blocks			
Dhariawad	2	7	45
Gogunda	1	4	37

Cont'd ...

Cont'd ...

Jhadol	1	6	54
Kherwada	2	8	73
Kotra	1	6	42
Salumber	1	7	52
Sarada	2	8	54
Non-tribal Blocks			
Badgaon	1	3	22
Bhinder	3	5	53
Girwa	1	10	54
Mavli	2	8	42
Tribal Area	**10**	**46**	**357**
Non-tribal Area	**7**	**26**	**171**
Total	**17**	**72**	**528**

Source: Office records maintained at the Office of CMHO, Udaipur (as on August 1997).

A comparison of available physical facilities with the standards indicates that the recommended norms have almost been achieved in case of physical infrastructure in the district.

The situation of health infrastructure is good in comparison with the norms prescribed by the Government of India. However, only the availability of physical infrastructure in quantitative terms is a necessary but not a sufficient condition for providing quality services. These buildings should be properly maintained for sustainable provision of quality services. While discussing with the district level officials it was noted that, although the buildings, through which the services are provided to the community (community health centres, primary health centres, and sub-centres), are adequate, they are in a poor state.

The most critical issues are water supply, sewage and sanitation within the buildings. The main reason for poor building condition is the non-existence of building maintenance. Most of the institutions need rewiring of electrical fittings. The availability of water supply is one of the major problems in these buildings. Even the community health centres and primary health centres collect water from bore wells and overhead tanks but in most of the facilities, the overhead tanks are in poor condition. Sometimes, the bore wells are not operational and sometimes the water is not safe for drinking.

The construction of the centre is defective at many places. Problems such as leaking of roofs, non-closing windows, and broken floors are not uncommon. The maintenance of cleanliness and hygiene in the health institutions is neglected. Even operation theatres and delivery rooms are not in clean and hygienic conditions. Toilets are always unclean, ill-maintained, and in many institutions (community health centres, primary health centres and sub-centres) non-operational.

For delivery of high quality services to the community, it is essential that a health centre has such basic amenities as appropriate building, electricity, water supply, and adequate space. A study carried out in Rajasthan for End-of-Project Evaluation of UNFPA Project Phase II (Gupta et al., 1996) observed that at sub-centres the buildings are in dilapidated conditions and do not often meet the standard norms. The concurrent evaluation observed that out of 930 sub-centres had covered under the study from the state (including all districts) only 37 and 41 per cent of sub-centres have electricity connection and water supply facilities respectively. In the study district, out of 30 sub-centres covered in the study, only 10, 37 and 40 per cent had water supply, residential quarters for staff, and electricity connection respectively.

Building maintenance is very poor and as a result, the infrastructure is not maintained. Even a minor repair is not undertaken which is the main contributing factor for the poor condition of the buildings. Maintenance of all the buildings and engineering services are executed by the public works department of state government which directs the respective funds. Requests by the health centres are to be sent to the public works department through a very long procedure and many a time the public works department does not even approach the health centre to initiate the work.

The district officials opined that a major problem in sub-centres is with the location (sub-centres are often located far away from the villages/market places), particularly, in tribal blocks of Kotra, Dhariyawad, Kherwara and Gogunda, which results in low attendance rates and staff absentees due to insecurity in the isolated areas. This results in poor contact of the health worker with the community and it affects the continuity of services, follow-up of the clients and interpersonal relations between clients and providers.

Drugs and Supplies

The routine supply of essential drugs to the health facilities in the district seems to be adequate, and no substantial lack of medicines and contraceptives has been reported by the district officials. The state government purchases drugs and supplies for the district from non-plan funds. The drugs are provided by the state government to the district, based on the demand received from the district. The district officials compile it on the basis of health institutions' demand. These are supplied to the districts. The chief medical and health officer decide the quantity of various drugs to be supplied to community health centres, primary health centres and sub-centres. The drugs and supplies are usually distributed every month to the health facilities. Shortage occurs sporadically due to procurement problems or mismatching of supplies from the district to actual local needs at the community health centre/primary health centre/sub-centre level. Distribution problems occur particularly during transfer of drugs from the primary health centres to sub-centre level. The sub-centre has to collect the allocated drug supplies from the primary health centres, through a process which is often impeded through long distances, lack of transport, and geographical situations of district in tribal areas.

The medical officers in-charge at primary health centres have a small fund at their disposal for purchasing additional essential drugs from the private market for emergency situations. The annual emergency drug fund at the community health centres level on an average is Rs 4,000 per month. It was also found that community health centres/primary health centres were supported with additional drugs by the private donations (rich families from the local villages). Drug donations, however, are irregular and not co-ordinated with the general supply procedures in the district.

The quantity of drugs to be distributed free of charge from various institutions has been doubled in the Eighth Plan in the state (Government of Rajasthan, 1990). In the year 1995–96 the state government has increased the budget for the health department by about 175 per cent which means that the availability of drugs at primary health centres and sub-centres is adequate (Srinivasan, 1996). The Government of India financed schemes and also pays for drugs and supplies for specific programmes such as family planning and mother and child health. This shows that the district is getting appropriate and adequate drugs and supplies of contraceptives required to run the programmes. A study of four states of India conducted by World Bank clearly indicates that the supplies are more adequate for vaccines/supplements and contraceptives (World Bank, 1995). The study of Rajasthan state by Government of Rajasthan observed that a majority of sub-centres (85%) and Udaipur (83%) have supplies of contraceptives (Government of Rajasthan, 1997).

Equipment

It was revealed during the discussions with the district officials that medical equipments at health care institutions in the district is less adequate than the supply of drugs and contraceptives. In most of the health institutions, equipment is either in poor condition or requiring maintenance.

The sub-centre plays an important role in providing the services in rural and tribal areas. The sub-centres are the first contact points for most of the clients in the rural and tribal areas. A client who demands maternal health services and family planning, first contacts the health worker at the sub-centre level for necessary services. Therefore, these sub-centres should be equipped with basic amenities to provide services. However, it was found that the equipment at sub-centres is not adequate. The concurrent evaluation observed that out of 930 sub-centres covered from the state under the study (including all districts), only the one-third have infant weighing scales, examination kit, delivery kit and urine examination facility. In the district, out of 30 sub-centres covered in the study, about 43–53 per cent had infant weighing scales, examination kit, delivery kit, and 17 per cent have urine examination facility. This situation affects the proper antenatal care of the pregnant women in rural areas.

IEC Material

The Information, Education and Communication (IEC) activities are important for demand generation of reproductive health services. The district is getting sufficient funds under Indian Population Project IX supported by UNFPA for organizing various activities to enhance awareness of communities for reproductive health services. The district health officials developed and disseminated a variety of materials including posters, pamphlets, magazine, etc.

Finance

The Government of Rajasthan allocates approximately 40 per cent of its total budget for the social service sector which includes education, medical health and family welfare, sanitation, water supply, housing, urban developments, and welfare of scheduled caste and tribes. The health sector ranks second in terms of budget allocation following education. The budget estimates for the medical and health department are usually presented in three categories non-plan, plan and centrally sponsored schemes. The share of salaries and wages constitutes 65.3 per cent and 72.3 per cent of the total expenditure for the years 1995–96 and 1994–95 respectively at the state level. This reflects, as in most of the other states, exorbitantly high recurring administrative costs.

Table 4.7

Revenue Expenditure for Medical, Health and Family Welfare in the Study District

(million Rs.)

	1995–96			*1994–95*		
Particular	*Non-plan*	*Plan*	*CSS*	*Non-plan*	*Plan*	*CSS*
Medical and Health	45.83	21.56	3.40	43.27	20.52	2.10
Family Welfare	0.25	1.96	26.00	0.22	0.69	33.20
Total	46.08	23.52	29.40	43.49	21.21	35.30

Source: Budget Documents, Directorate of Medical, Health and Family Welfare Services, Government of Rajasthan, 1991–95.

The problems in the state are as well reflected in the scenario with respect to the health care financing in the study district. Due to concentration of tribal population in the district, the Government of Rajasthan as well as the Government of India have special interest in the socio-economic development of this district. It received the following budget (Table 4.7) during 1995–96 and 1994–95, which is quite low, in spite of the fact that the health status of the district is poor in comparison to that of other developed districts.

Clients

Clients are very important inputs in the health care system. Clients in the present system have been defined as narrowly as "15–45 years married eligible women". This definition is not *in keeping with* reproductive health approach. The reproductive health approach focuses on assisting individuals of any age group in meeting their personal reproductive health goals. Moreover, to provide quality of care to clients of family planning services, informed choice is one of the elements of quality, which says that client's inputs are very much necessary for the provider. Again, the provider has to supply complete information to the clients before providing the services. For this, the provider has to get an assurance from the clients by asking whether they have understood properly or not about the services. Clients' satisfaction is also necessary for providing quality of care. It was observed from the concurrent evaluation data that the providers are not using effectively and efficiently the clients as input. However, as per the discussion with the district level officials, it is highly manipulable for improving the quality of care in the district.

From the above analysis it is clear that there are various input factors which have contributed to the current level of the quality of care of reproductive health services in the district. But all the factors are not at the same level of importance, favourablity, and manipulability.

Table 4.8

Assessment of Inputs

Factors	*Important*	*Adequacy*	*Manipulability*
Number of doctors at CHC/PHC Level	3	3	3
Number of staff at sub-centre level	3	4	1
Filled-in positions of personnel in tribal areas	5	1	4
Manpower trained in interpersonal relations	5	1	4
Number of health facilities	4	4	1
Basic amenities at health facilities	3	1	2
Location of health facility building in village	2	2	1
Regular supply	2	3	2
Distribution of supplies	1	3	3
Minimum necessary equipments	4	3	2
Maintenance of building/equipment	1	2	3
Clients	4	2	4

Table 4.8 provides an analysis of the factors in terms of their adequacy (the extent to which the factor makes a positive contribution), Importance (how important the factor is in influencing the quality of care), and manipulability (how easy it is to influence the factor). The scoring of adequacy and importance are done on the basis of findings of other researches reported in the literature, data collected from the district and the researcher's intuitive judgement, and of the manipulability on the basis of discussions with the district level officials. The rating for each factor has been done on a five-point scale (1–5), where 1 denotes the lowest value and 5 denotes the highest value. A system of rating is used so that no more than 20 per cent items secure the same score. This is done to ensure greater degree of discrimination in scoring.

Information

The fourth component of Jain's Diagnostic Model is *information.* The manager needs up-to-date, reliable, and complete information on all the other components (*desired output/actual output, environment, inputs, and process*) of the system, in order to make well-informed management decisions about the performance and operations of the programme for effective management of the system. This permits the system to adjust, to cope with, and to benefit from all new developments. Comprehensive, accurate, and sensitive information is vital not only for the effective and efficient functioning of the system, but also for its very survival. It should constantly and accurately monitor all developments in all components of the system and transmit all relevant information to all concerned parties. The manager relies on information generated both inside the system (internal) and outside the system (external). The information is communicated through formal (officials) and informal (unofficial) channels. The managers rely on both informal and formal ways of obtaining the information they need to make decisions:

Internal Formal	These reports, which are generally standardized in format and produced on a regular basis, constitute the most visible part of what is called the management information system.
Internal Informal	Peers, subordinates, superiors, rumours, gossips.
External Formal	Publications (journals, newspapers), conferences, evaluation report, census reports, research report, reports by other departments of concern, students working on the same problem, and mass media reports, etc.
External Informal	Outside members [physicians, customers, suppliers, bankers, persons in associated organizations, non-members (outside business and professional associates), others (chance encounters, neighbours).

Informal information includes rumours and unofficial discussions with colleagues. Personal experience, education, common sense, intuition, and knowledge of the political and social situation are also part of the informal means of gathering information. In contrast, formal information usually reaches managers in the form the routine statistical and management reports. The relative importance of these channels varies greatly from programme to programme, culture to culture, and time to time.

Information Needs

The system needs information on all other components of the system to make decisions about planning, monitoring and evaluating the quality of services. The system needs information about the current level of performance with respect to desired output; about the environmental situation contributing to the achievement of the desired output, about inputs situation to achieve the desired output, and about the processor and the processing parts of the system to achieve the desired output. The system needs information on quality of care elements: method of choice, information given to clients, interpersonal relations, technical competence of provider, follow-up mechanism for continuity, and appropriate constellation of services. The system provides clinic-based contraceptives: IUD and sterilization, it needs to collect information on side effects and complications. In brief, all these items of information are required to achieve the desired output.

Types of Available Information

The type of information that is currently available through monthly reports of primary health centres are as follows: eligible couples contacted, operations done (vasectomy and tubectomy); sterilization cases followed up (contacted upto previous month, complications reported, and deaths); IUD insertions; IUD cases followed up (contacted upto month, complications reported, and discontinued IUD: removed, expelled); oral pills cycles (total women on pills at the beginning of the month, total women initiated to pills during the month, total women reported complications, total discontinued during the month, and distributed by primary health centre); *Nirodh* pieces distributed; medical termination of pregnancy (number performed, follow-up, complications reported, acceptors of family planning methods).

The above information is generated at the sub-centre level and transmitted to the primary health centre level at monthly intervals. At the primary health centre level, the medical officer in-charge review the performance of the sub-centres and compiles a detailed report incorporating the primary health centre performance, which is transmitted to the block primary health centre. At block primary health centre, a detailed report is compiled, including the performance reports received from primary health centres, and the same is forwarded to the district level.

Monthly reports are a very important modes of monitoring the programme. They provide data which can be converted into useful information for monitoring not only the physical progress but also the quality of the programme. However, these monthly reports do not provide information on the quality aspect.

If accuracy and timeliness of the reports are ensured at supervisory levels, it can become the most effective method of managing the programme. The reports lose their effectiveness as a monitoring tool if these are not analysed in time by superiors in position to provide feedback to their subordinates. In the existing management information system, the staff at the sub-centre level is overburdened with recordkeeping, and spends about 30 per cent of the office hours in maintaining the records. Registers are available to collect and record the information at the sub-centre level for each village. The registers are kept at the sub-centre level. The report formats are available for each level, i.e., sub-centre and primary health centre level. The registers are available with almost all the sub-centres. However, these are not updated regularly, which leads to incomplete and inadequate information for programme planning and management. The Concurrent Evaluation of Reproductive Health and Child Care in Rajasthan conducted by the Government of Rajasthan during 1996–97, observed that out of 30 sub-centres from the district covered under the study, about 27 per cent of the ANMs were not making correct entries in the service delivery register and about 50 per cent were not sending correct monthly reports to the primary health centre level. This reflects the extent of inadequacy and inaccuracy of the data available to the system manager in the district, which leads to poor quality of data for appropriate planning and management available to the system manager. Analysis and use of data for problem assessment, problem solving and planning purposes is not performed at any level in the district. Feedback to the primary level is not provided on the data they submit. It leads to falsification of data transmitted from lower level to higher level. Records are not maintained to monitor and follow-up referred patients.

The auxiliary nurse midwife also collects data for eligible couple register every year. In the eligible couple register, the following data are collected:

1. Name of village, household number and couple number.
2. Name of eligible couple: Husband, wife, religion and caste.
3. Age of husband and wife.
4. Number of children (male and female).
5. Age (in years and months) and sex of youngest child.
6 Whether the woman had delivered during the previous calendar year (1 January to 31 December). If yes, the

following details are recorded: where the delivery took place; who conducted the delivery; whether tetanus toxoid vaccination was received; Whether iron and folic acid tablets were received; outcome of the delivery; if child is alive, present age of the child (in months); if dead, age at the time of death (in months and days).

7. Whether any maternal death happened in the household during the previous calendar year.
8. If the age of the youngest child is less than one year, whether the following vaccinations were received: BCG, DPT (I, II, III), Polio (I, II, III), measles. vitamin A; whether the immunization card is available.
9. Whether the woman is pregnant, and if so, date of last menstrual period and expected date of delivery; IFA tablets (number); TT vaccinations (number), and status of pregnancy.
10. If the woman is not pregnant, whether she desires more children, if yes, when.
11. If the woman is not pregnant, whether she/her husband had adopted any method of family planning methods; if not, reasons; if yes, the name of the method; whether the couple is satisfied with the use of this family planning method.

The above information is also not enough with respect to the quality of services. These are not adequate for the system manager. The Directorate of Medical, Health and Family Welfare Services, Government of Rajasthan, initiated some efforts to prepare and compile a demographic data base at the district level on the basis of information collected by auxiliary nurse midwives for eligible couple registers. For the study district, it was found that the information was grossly inadequate and incomplete on the following aspects of eligible couple register immunization of children, type of assistance at the time of delivery, childhood mortality, satisfaction with the family planning method being used by the couples (Goyal et al., 1996).

Another problem with the existing information system is that it provides data on maternal deaths only on the basis of hospital records. But, in the district, a majority of the population is characterized by tribes living in rural and remote areas in hilly and forest regions, facing the problem of inaccessibility of health services. Hence, most of the maternal deaths go unreported, as the programme is not responsive to the other sources of information like, non-governmental organizations, the community, private medical practitioners, media, etc. Therefore, it can be concluded that the figures of the deaths due to reproductive health matters in the district are not realistic and adequate, timely, and accurate. The records and reports are part of a ritual rather than a useful tool. The reports are not analysed and interpreted for decision-making at the local level, not even at the district level.

The concurrent evaluation generates information needed by the system for monitoring quality of services, i.e., method of choice, information given to clients, interpersonal relations, technical competence of provider, follow-up/mechanism for continuity, and appropriate constellation of services. However, the concurrent evaluation provides limited information on these aspects. The evaluation does not provide any information on environment, and very limited information on other parts of the system. The system may generate information through external informal sources, but it was found through discussion with key personnel in the district that it was not adequate, though it might be very useful.

Table 4.9

Assessment of Information

Factors	*Important*	*Adequacy*	*Quality*	*Manipulability*
Service statistics reliability	5	3	3	5
Comprehensiveness	4	1	1	4
Eligible couple register	2	2	2	3
Concurrent evaluation	3	4	4	2

From the above analysis, it is clear that there are various factors in the information component of Jain's Diagnostic Model which are influencing the quality of care in the district. But, all the factors are different in terms of their adequacy, quality, importance and manipulability. Table 4.9 provides an analysis of these factors in terms of their importance, adequacy, quality, and manipulability. The rating for each factor has been done on a five-point scale (1–5), where 1 denotes the lowest value and 5 denotes the highest value.

Process

The fifth box in Jain's Diagnostic Model is the process. It is the most important box. The desired output (DO) is achieved through the process. It achieves the desired output by manipulating all other boxes. It has the following two components: processor and processing.

Processor

The key players of the system, who are in a position or have the power/authority to achieve the desired output are called processors. In the present study, the processors are identified at three levels: district, block and sub-centre levels.

Table 4.10

Identification of Key Processors at Various Levels of the System

Level	*Processor*
District	Chief Medical and Health Officer
	Deputy Chief Medical and Health Officer (Family Welfare)
	Maternal and Child Health (MCH) Officer
Block/PHC	Medical Officer In-charge
Sub-Centre	Auxiliary Nurse Mid-wife (ANM)

The chief medical and health officer, the deputy chief medical and health officer (family welfare) and the maternal and child health officer, together are responsible for planning and implementing various activities of the reproductive health services at the district level. At block level (primary health centre/community health centre), the medical officer in-charge is the processor, and at the sub-centre level, the auxiliary nurse-midwife. The characteristics which impacting the processor in processing is measured in this study by the three Cs:

- Concern for quality services
- Competence for providing quality services
- Continuity with health system

Concern for Quality Services: The concern for quality of care may be reflected by two elements of quality of care framework: choice of method and information given to clients. The concurrent evaluation reveals that in the district only 57 per cent of the clients were given a method choice at the time of adopting the family planning method, only 5 per cent were told about possible side effects, 2 per cent about both the advantages and disadvantages of the method, 12 per cent were advised about periodic check-ups, and 8 per cent on proper breast feeding. This shows the low level of concern for providing quality services.

Table 3.1 shows that in the study district only 16 per cent of the spacing method users were told about regular follow-up visits, and only 1 per cent of the spacing method users were told about to report the health worker in case of any side effect. Table 3.1 also shows that about 49 per cent of the current users of spacing methods received a follow-up visit by the provider within a month, and about 79 per cent of the sterilization clients received a follow-up visits after adoption of the method. In case of maternal health services, only 12 per cent of the women received at least three visits during their antenatal period and about 27 per cent of them received a follow-up visit by health worker during the postnatal period within a week after delivery.

The low concern for quality of services is also reflected in the fact that, many a time, the primary health centre medical officer working in remote areas visits the primary health centre only at long intervals to get his salary. The general attitude among the workers and the doctors is that they are servants of the government, and so they are responsible for serving their supervisors rather than the clients. The incumbent at each level tries to keep his supervisor happy, rather than support his subordinates in their functions to serve the clients. Practically, this tantamounts to neglecting the clients, compromising safety standards in performing procedures, and, at times, work is done only on paper. At each level, the processor almost never discusses the quality of care in any meeting, reflecting the low level of his concern. They discuss only targets and achievements.

The infrastructural problems are not only those of civil engineering and physical maintenance, but also of attitude, habits, and behaviour, which reflect the lack of concern for quality of care. This does not require much by way of additional resources. However, it calls for the concern of the staff for quality. There are instances of excellent maintenance, where the doctor-in-charge in particular has taken keen interest in ensuring it. Hence, the lack of systematic management as well as individual initiative contributes to the poor infrastructure facilities in the primary health care system.

Competence for Providing Quality Services: The processor requires certain competencies, technical and behavioural, for providing quality services. The district level processor should be competent to manage various aspects of competence, i.e., competence of the clinical technique of providers, the observance of protocols, and meticulous asepsis required to provide clinical family planning methods and safe motherhood services. Discussions with district level officials revealed that they do not practice any method to manage the above competencies, that is, they are not competent. To assess the competence of the medical officer in-charge and auxiliary nurse midwife, the data used is based on whether the provider offered services that are expected as part of a competent service (as defined by an obstetrician/gynecologist, rather than by the actual quality of the services provided). In terms of measures of technical competence in family planning services, whether the provider inquired about the clients' health problems and menstruation status at the time of adoption, and whether the necessary examinations had been performed by the provider, are taken into account. Table 3.1 shows that only 36 per cent of the clients were enquired about their general health problems, and 22 per cent about their menstruation cycle, before providing the method. Moreover, 21 per cent clients reported that blood pressure reading was taken by the health worker at the time of adopting family planning method, and by 22 per cent that vaginal and breast examinations were performed at the time of adopting the family planning method.

The technical competence of the provider, in case of maternal health services, is assessed on the various activities the worker is expected to perform for a pregnant woman for better care. These include: (i) taking medical history (obstetric history, general health, weight and height, calculating the expected date of delivery, and assessing risk factors); (ii) examination (general physical, obstetric and edema); and (iii) enquiring about bleeding/pain in abdomen. Table 3.1 indicates that only 3 per cent of women reported that obstetric history was noted, only five per cent that general health problems were inquired about, about 42 per cent that weight and height were recorded, about 40 per cent that expected date of delivery was worked out, and 40 per cent that risk factors were assessed for them during the antenatal period.

Moreover, 57 per cent of the women reported about general physical examination, 8 per cent about obstetric examination, and 61 per cent about edema examination, having been performed by the health worker during their antenatal period. About 68 per cent of the women reported that they were inquired about bleeding/pain in abdomen during the antenatal period.

Continuity with the System: Continuity means the length of service of the processor. It is an important quality for system's better performance, since, if the processor is changed, every thing would change, i.e., desired output, strategy, plan, etc. Discussion with the district level officials revealed that there are no policies or guidelines of the government regarding transfer and promotion. There is high political interference in posting and transferring officials and even in changing the portfolio of programme managers at district level. It results in low motivation of the officials in making any efforts to provide quality of care.

There are no policy guidelines that the district level officials would not be transferred before a minimum period of services, say 3–5 years.

Table 4.11

Assessment of the Processor's Characteristics (3 Cs)

Processors	*Impor-tant*	*Concern*		*Competence*		*Continuity*		*Average*	
		Current Status	Mani-pula-bility	Current Status	Mani-pula-bility	Current Status	Mani-pula-bility	Current Status	Mani-pula-bility
CMHO	3	1	3	1	2	3	1	1.6	2
Dy. CMHO (FW)	5	2	4	2	5	4	2	2.6	3.6
MCHO	5	2	4	2	5	2	2	2	3.6
MOIC	4	2	4	2	4	3	2	2.3	3.3
ANM	4	2	4	2	5	4	2	2.6	3.6

The person who has had good years of experience in one programme gets suddenly transferred to another programme. This shows ineffective planning at the district level for posting and transfers. At the community health centre/primary health centre level, the post of medical officer-in-charge is also subject to political interference. A study done in Udaipur district by Government of Rajasthan shows that, at sub-centre level, the auxiliary nurse midwife is less affected by frequent transfers, only about 10 per cent of the auxiliary nurse midwives in the district had one transfer in the last five year period (Government of Rajasthan, 1997).

Processing

Processing is a function, which achieves the desired output by manipulating all other boxes. Processing is performed by various processors to achieve the desired output. It has two parts: manipulation of all components of the system and implementation.

Manipulation of the Desired Output: The processor could not manipulate the desired output in the district. He received the feedback report from the state government about the quality of services being provided in the district, but did not make any special efforts to improve the services. The desired output can be manipulated first by clarity of the desired output and then by setting measurable indicators.

Manipulation of Environment: Manipulation of environment relates to the processor's efforts in making hostile factors less hostile and friendly factors more friendly towards improving the quality of services. In manipulating the environmental factors, the processor has not been able to manipulate effectively the policy changes of the Government of Rajasthan, which have influenced the programme at the district level. The processor initiated many activities to involve private medical practitioners and non-governmental organizations in providing reproductive health services. However, the focus should be on quality of care, which can be influenced by training private medical practitioners and non-governmental organizations in quality of care. The *processor* has not been successful in manipulating community participation, non-governmental organizations, and inter-sectoral convergence effectively. The funding agencies are in favour of providing funds for quality improvement, but in the district, the processor could not generate additional funds for quality improvement.

Manipulation of Inputs: Regarding the manipulation of inputs in terms of manpower, the processor has somehow been able to influence this factor. Still, the tribal population are served poorly in spite of the fact that the government is expected to provide additional assistance to these areas for improving their health status. The processor has not been able to manipulate the location of these health facilities effectively. With regard to equipment, the processor could not obtain it in adequate quantity from the state government. Udaipur district, as part of the tribal sub-plan, receives special attention from the central and state governments for improving the socio-economic status of the community. The commissioner (tribal welfare), who is stationed in Udaipur, has some funds earmarked for health care activities. The commissioner (tribal welfare) also supports projects related to mother and child health and family welfare, undertaken by non-governmental organizations working in tribal pockets. In 1995–96, about 10 per cent of the tribal development budget was spent on health measures, mainly for renovation of health facilities and purchase of equipment/drugs. Even this could not be mobilized by the processor properly due to lack of co-ordination between the two offices. The clients are very important inputs in providing client-centred quality services. However, the processors could not manipulate them effectively. Clients' involvement can be increased in various forms to improve the quality of the services.

Manipulation of Information: Manipulation of information relates to setting up of a system of providing timely, reliable and accurate information, and use of the information in making corrections to achieve the desired output. The processor has failed to manipulate the information favourably. Under an external aided project, a computer was installed at the district level. However, the processor could not manipulate the existing computer for data processing, storage of data and monitoring for the programme.

The information can be manipulated by using service statistics in data analysis at each level and making corrective actions. Monitoring of quality indicators may be done in the district. The existing system of data collection may be strengthened by establishing a mechanism for verification. Moreover, the monthly meetings at block level, which are attended by the district level officials, may be used for monitoring the quality, rather than making the meeting a mere ritual.

Manipulation of Processor: There are evidences that the district health officials participated in a training programme conducted by the State Institute of Health and Family Welfare, Jaipur, under India Population Project during 1996. The training programme focused on modern management concepts and methods, improved health care delivery system, finances and personnel administration. The district health officials also participated in a workshop on *leadership and management development for reproductive health programmes in India* jointly organized by International Council on Management of Population Programmes, Malaysia and Indian Institute of Health Management Research, Jaipur during September 29 – October 4, 1997 at Jaipur. However, the processor at district level seems to be less competent in managing quality of care. These are not sufficient for the processors in managing the quality of care. The processors may be manipulated by providing training on planning for quality, the development of objective for quality, setting standards (including guidelines, protocols, etc.), actively communicating standards, developing indicators, setting thresholds, collecting data to monitor compliance with standards and applying solutions to improve reproductive health of the community.

Table 4.12

Assessment of Processing (Manipulation of all Components)

Manipulation	*Important*	*Current Status*	*Manipulability*
Desired Output	5	1	5
Environment	3	2	3
Inputs	3	3	2
Information	4	2	4
Processor	5	1	5

Implementation Issues: Implementation includes many aspects, such as: prevalent strategy and its soundness, implementation planning, operation management, monitoring, motivating, etc.

Prevalent Strategy and its Soundness: After careful search of government documents at the district level and discussions with the district level officials, who are directly involved in planning and implementation of reproductive health services in the district, it was observed that there is absence of a strategy for improving quality of care in the district. For improving quality of services, a sound strategy should be in place.

Implementation Planning: There is no plan as such for providing quality of care. In the district, reproductive and child health plans have been developed for 1995–96, 1996–97 and 1997–98. The planning process was initiated at the village and sub-centre levels aggregated at the primary health centre level for respective areas, and summarized in the district plan for family planning and maternal health services. This exercise is mainly putting together a set of data and information with regard to population, coverage and achievement of services. Targets for the plan year are identified. At the district level, Information, Education and Communication (IEC) plan is also formulated for communication and information planning. These are not focused on the quality of care. No training plan is developed in the district for the staff to provide quality services.

It has been observed that the system conducts the *eligible couple survey* during April-June of every year, which is carried out by auxiliary nurse midwives posted at sub-centre level. On the basis of the data collected in the survey for each village, a service delivery register is prepared by the health worker. The need for family planning, and maternal and child health services was assessed during the survey, and the couples were divided into the following segments, and entries in the service register made accordingly: (1) couples who are current users of spacing methods and couples who have "unmet need" for spacing methods (couples who do not want a child for a period of two years and above); (2) couples who have "unmet need" for limiting methods (couples who do not want more children); (3) couples who have two or more children but are not inclined to adopt any method; (4) couples who need antenatal care; and (5) couples who need postnatal care.

Monitoring: Effective monitoring is the key to the success of a programme. The monitoring of a programme is expected to be done in three ways: supervision through field visits, reporting meeting and periodical meetings. Field visits by supervisors are intended to supervise the work of the field functionaries by superiors, help them overcome problems in effective discharge of their functions, reviewing the performance and giving them guidance and support to improve and also to interact with the community to assess the satisfaction level of services provided. To achieve this, the following norms are prescribed for field visits: the maternal and child health officer and deputy chief medical and health officer (family welfare) are expected to visit at least three poorly performing primary health centres, five sub-centres and two post-partum centres in the district to have on the spot assessment of the activities, find out service delivery gaps and take corrective actions. During these visits, the service delivery units in inaccessible and remote areas shall be monitored closely with the concerned medical officers responsible for this. Both the officers should visit the poorly performing institutions and after ascertaining the reasons for poor performance, should take corrective steps to improve performance during the next month. This visit should result in improvement of performance by the next month. At the primary health centre level, the medical officer in-charge is expected to pay a surprise visit to one or two sub-centres each month to supervise their activities, and also for interacting with the community, *Jan Mangal* volunteers and *Sarpanchas*.

The block health supervisors (male and female) are expected to visit at least 15 villages with low couple protection rate or high infant mortality rate and maternal mortality rate as per the district action plan per month and carry out intensive information education and communication activities. The extension and publicity officer is expected to participate in the activities of at least 10 villages per month along with block education extensor and block health supervisor (female) in the villages having resistant populations. This monitoring is also not being performed regularly in the district due to shortage of block health supervisors (male and female) and the extension and publicity officer not having a jeep for travelling, though he can use the matador for this purpose. But, this is not convenient in the district due to its geographical situation.

At the district level, there is no arrangement for evaluation of the quality of services being rendered by the health care institutions in the district. Therefore, in the existing system, the monitoring and evaluation of the programme performance in terms of quality of care is totally absent. The district health system has to conduct rapid assessment methods to know the status of quality of care.

Coordination: It has been observed in the district that there has been weak coordination among the district health officials in planning, managing, and implementing activities for improving quality of reproductive health services. Since all services are delivered in an integrated package, due to poor co-ordination among the district level processors, the processors at the primary health centre and at the sub-centre levels are unable to provide quality services. Furthermore, lack of linkages and co-ordination between primary and secondary level institutions in the district leads to poor referral.

Motivation: There is no harm if the providers do not provide quality services, and nor rewarded if they do so. Therefore, to improve the quality of services there should be well-established risk (for not providing services, as per quality standard) and rewards (for providing services as per quality standard). The following table depicts the importance, current status, and manipulability on a five point-scale of each of the factors related to implementation:

Table 4.13

Assessment of Processing (Implementation Issues)

Implementation Issues	*Important*	*Current Status*	*Manipulability*
Sound strategy	5	1	5
Implementation planning	4	2	4
Monitoring	3	2	5
Coordination	3	3	4
Motivation	4	1	5

CHAPTER 5

Formulating Strategy for Quality Improvement

Concept of Strategy

In the previous chapter, we made an effort to determine the factors responsible for the current state of quality of care in the district, using Jain's Diagnostic Model. In this chapter, an effort is made to formulate a strategy to improve the quality of care in the district. 'Strategy' is a single unified approach, which addresses only those who will make a difference (Jain, 1997). Strategy is the means that an organization chooses to move from where it is today to a desired state, sometime in the future as depicted in the Figure 5.1.

Figure 5.1
Strategy Links Today with Tomorrow

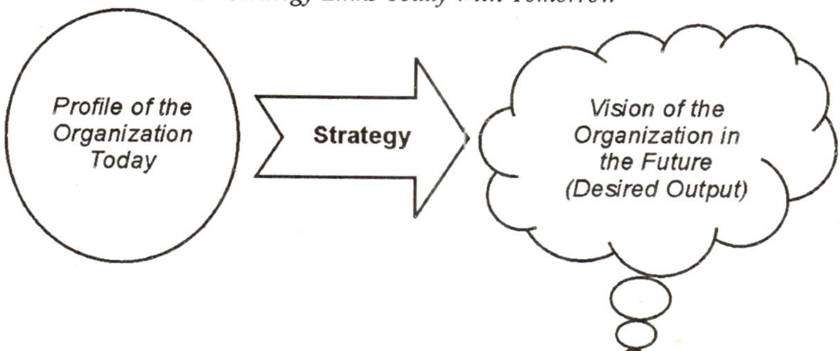

The strategy may be viewed as the sum of the forces in the environment, and suggests "what the organization should do" and is also influenced by the capabilities of the organization and represents "what the organization can do". The consistency of the behaviour is "driven" by a set of common organizational values and goals. The values and goals are often the result of considerable analysis by top management and indicate, "what the organization wants to do". When management considers all these forces and develops a series of consistent top-level decisions, the organization can be said to have a strategy. The requirements of decision consistency suggest that a strategy is the means of an organization chooses to move from where it is today to a desired state sometime in the future. Thus, the strategy also may be viewed as a set of guidelines or a plan that will help assure consistency in decision-making (Duncan et al., 1995).

Figure 5.2

Strategy as Interaction, Integration and Result of System's Components

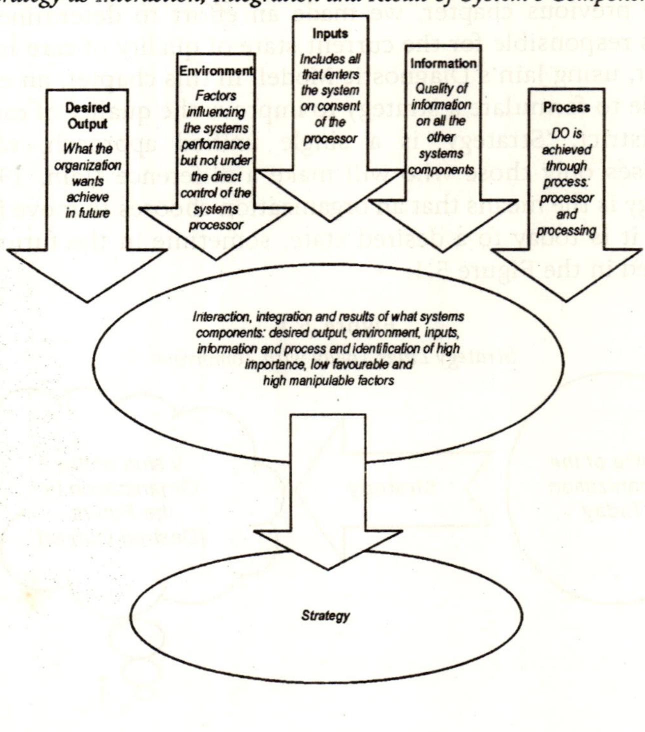

The strategy is thus the means of achieving the desired or expected position for the organization sometime in future. The strategy is not a one-step trajectory to achieve desired position but rather involves a hierarchy of decisions, each taken to move towards the desired position in the future. The decisions taken must be unified towards achieving the desired goal.

Strategic management and the development of a strategy are essential parts of a decision-making process, making a choice from several strategic alternatives. Therefore, strategy formulation is not a single decision, rather a series of increasingly specific decisions.

Formulating Strategy

System's diagnosis, considered in Chapter 4, involves a great deal of gathering data, classifying, and understanding information, and contains a comprehensive investigation of the factors responsible for the current performance of quality of care, from among the five components of the model (*desired output, environment, inputs, information, and process*). As illustrated in Figure 5.2 the interaction, integration and result of these components form the basis for the development of the strategy. These interrelated components drive the strategy. The five components of Jain's Diagnostic Model simultaneously affect the formulation of a strategy and provide input to the strategy.

In each component these factors are not at the same level of: (i) *importance* (in case of all five components); *favourability* (in case of desired output and environment), adequacy (in case of inputs and information); *current status* (in case of processors and processing); and *manipulability* (in case of all components). Table 5.1 summarizes the information on these factors (for each system component) in terms of their *importance* (how important the factor is in influencing the quality of care), *favourability/adequacy/current status* (the extent to which the factor makes a positive contribution), and *manipulability* (how easy it is to influence the factor), based on the analysis presented in Chapter 4. The rating for each factor in each component has been done on a five-point scale (1–5), where 1 denotes the lowest value and 5 denotes the highest value.

Table 5.1

Summary of Factors Analysed through Diagnostic Model

Factors			
Desired Output	*Importance*	*Favourability*	*Manipulability*
Clarity of Desired Output	5	1	5
Environment	*Importance*	*Favourability*	*Manipulability*
Physical characteristics	2	1	1
Socio-economic status	2	3	2
Resistant community	2	3	4
Tribal population	1	1	2
Density of population	1	1	1
Transport development	3	3	2
Communication development	3	4	3
Regulation for private medical practitioners	4	2	5
State government support	5	5	3
Donors' interest	1	4	3
Research/training institution	3	4	4
Role of non-governmental organizations	4	2	5
State policy	5	3	3
Political interference	4	3	2
Inputs	*Important*	*Adequacy*	*Manipulability*
Number of doctors at CHC/PHC level	3	3	3
Number of staff at SC level	3	4	1
Filled posts of personnel in tribal areas	5	1	4
Manpower trained in interpersonal skills	5	1	4
Number of health facilities	4	4	1
Basic amenities at health facilities	3	1	2

Cont'd ...

Cont'd ...

Location of building in village	2	2		1
Regular supply	2	3		2
Distribution	1	3		3
Minimum necessary equipments	4	3		2
Maintenance of building/equipment	1	2		3
Clients	4	2		4
Information	*Important*	*Adequacy*	*Quality*	*Manipulability*
Service statistics reliability	5	3	3	5
Comprehensiveness	4	1	1	4
Eligible couple register	2	2	2	3
Concurrent evaluation	3	4	4	2
Process	*Important*	*Current Status*		*Manipulability*
Processors				
3 Cs of CMHO	3	1.6		2
3 Cs of Deputy CMHO (Family Welfare)	5	2.6		3.6
3 Cs of MCH Officer	5	2		3.6
3 Cs of Medical Officer	4	2.3		3.3
3 Cs of ANM	4	2.6		3.6
Processing				
Manipulation of Desired Output	5	1		5
Manipulation of environment	3	2		3
Manipulation of inputs	3	3		2
Manipulation of information	4	2		4
Manipulation of processor	5	1		5
Soundness of strategy	5	1		5
Implementation planning	4	2		4
Monitoring	3	2		5
Coordination	3	3		4
Motivation	4	1		5

Jain's Diagnostic Model requires us to concentrate on those factors of the problem that most deserve attention and desires a focused attempt at a resolution. The first step in this direction is to select only those factors, which are highly important in influencing the quality of care (those which scored 4 or 5 on the five-point scale), irrespective of their score on favourability and manipulability. The next step is to identify the factors (among the highly important ones) which are low favourability (which scored less than 3 on the five-point scale), and highly manipulable (which scored more than 3 on the five-point scale). By doing so, we get those factors which are highly important, low favourability and highly manipulable. Table 5.2 presents highly important, low favourability and highly manipulable factors identified.

Table 5.2

Identification of High Importance, Low Favourablity and Highly Manipulable Factors

Factors	*High I*	*Low F/A/CS*	High M
DO	*Important*	*Favourability*	*Manipulability*
Clarity of DO	5	1	5
Environment	*Important*	*Favourability*	*Manipulability*
Regulation for private medical practitioner	4	2	5
Role of non-governmental organizations	4	2	5
Inputs	*Important*	*Adequacy*	*Manipulability*
Filled posts of personnel in tribal areas	5	1	4
Manpower trained in interpersonal skills	5	1	4
Clients	4	2	4

Cont'd ...

Cont'd ...

Information	*Important*	*Adequacy*	*Quality*	*Manipulability*
Service statistics reliability	5	3	3	5
Comprehensiveness	4	1	1	4
Process	*Important*	*Current Status*		*Manipulability*
Processors				
3 Cs of Deputy CMHO (FW)	5	2.6		3.6
3 Cs of MCH Officer	5	2		3.6
3 Cs of Medical Officer	4	2.3		3.3
3 Cs of ANM	4	2.6		3.6
Processing				
Manipulation of Desired Output	5	1		5
Manipulation of information	4	2		4
Manipulation of processor	5	1		5
Soundness of strategy	5	1		5
Implementation planning	4	2		4
Motivation	4	1		5

It provides a logical and consistent conceptual framework for analysing these decisions. These decisions will result in a strategy for the organization. This strategy will be the guiding strategy, which provides general guidance and direction to the system, and is, therefore, called guiding strategy. Table 5.2 suggests that there are a few critical factors affecting the quality of care in the district, which are of high degree of importance, low degree of favourability/ adequacy/current status, and high degree of manipulability. The most important of them is the system not setting any desired output for quality of care of reproductive health services. High performance systems tend to have a firm statement on the desired output. Further, this statement tends to be clear, precise, measurable, and acceptable to all major stakeholders. Therefore, in the present system, the guiding strategy would be to establish a sound desired output for quality of care of reproductive health services in the district, assuming the project period to be of three years.

Strategy

Establish a sound desired output (DO) for quality of care of reproductive health services.

To achieve this strategy, we have to set a sound desired output for quality of care of reproductive health services in the district. As discussed in Chapter 3, the overall indicators' score for quality of care in the district worked out to be 37, is the Actual Output (AO). The Desired Output (DO), which should be realistic, precise and measurable and time bound may be stated as follows:

Desired Output

To achieve the quality of care at the level of 50 (overall score) by the end of the project.

The following indicators shall be used to measure the overall indicators score for quality of care in the district at the time of monitoring and evaluation:

Elements of Quality of Care	*Indicators*
Choice of methods	Per cent of clients told about methods other than the one accepted at the time of adoption.
Information given to clients	Per cent of clients told about side effects of method at the time of adoption of family planning method.
	Per cent of clients told about risk of method at the time of adoption of family planning method.
	Per cent of clients told about both advantages and disadvantages of the method at the time of adoption of family planning method.
	Per cent of clients advised on periodic check-up during antenatal period.
	Per cent of clients advised on use of safe delivery kit (*Mamta* kit) in case of home delivery.

Cont'd ...

Cont'd ...

	Per cent of clients advised on proper breast feeding to infants during postnatal period.
Technical competence	Per cent of clients inquired about general health problems and menstruation before providing family planning method.
	Per cent of clients for whom examinations were performed for blood pressure, vagina, and breast before providing family planning method.
	Per cent of clients for whom medical history was (obstetric history, general health, weight and height, expected date of delivery worked out, risk factors assessed) taken during antenatal period.
	Per cent of clients for whom examinations were performed for general physical health, obstetric problems and edema during antenatal period.
	Per cent of clients inquired about bleeding/pain in abdomen during antenatal care.
Interpersonal relations	Per cent of clients visited at home during previous three months.
	Per cent of clients satisfied with the assistance provided by health worker during home visit.
Mechanisms to encourage continuity	Per cent of clients who were informed about the precautions and regular follow-up/check-up.
	Per cent of clients informed about reporting in case of side-effects/complication.
	Per cent of clients received follow-up after adopting spacing method.
	Per cent of clients who received follow-up after sterilization.
	Per cent of clients received at least three visits during antenatal care.
	Per cent of clients who received postnatal care visit within a week after delivery.
Appropriate constellation of services	Per cent of health facilities that offers family planning, safe motherhood, reproductive tract infection and sexually transmitted diseases services on daily basis.
	Per cent of providers carrying out sexually transmitted diseases counselling to safe motherhood/family planning clients.

After developing the guiding strategy, and stating the desired output and the indicators to measure the desired output, consideration is given to the adaptive strategies. Next, more specific strategic decisions will have to be made. These decisions include determination of the adaptive strategy, market entry strategy, and the positioning strategy. The general strategy of the system is developed on the basis of these decisions.

To achieve the above-mentioned desired output, we have to improve those factors which affect the quality most. According to Jain's Diagnostic Model and also as reflected in Table 5.2, improving the key human resources will have the most effect. Therefore, the concern for quality and competence of the provider to after quality services have to be enhanced to improve the quality of care of reproductive health services.

Jain's Diagnostic Model provides in-depth and detailed information concerning the five components of the system, i.e., *desired output, environment, inputs, information, and process,* which are used in formulating the guiding strategy. The result of system diagnosis is also used to develop strategic alternatives and select the strategy for the system. Operational strategies then may be developed to implement the broader organizational strategy. The adaptive strategies are central to the strategy formulation process and are the broadest interpretation of the guiding strategy. Several methods are available to help managers think about adaptive strategic decisions: a threats, opportunities, weaknesses, and strength (TOWS) matrix; product life cycle analysis; portfolio analysis; extended portfolio matrix analysis; strategic position and action evaluation (SPACE); and programme evaluation (Duncan et al., 1995).

In our example of study district, we are using the following methods to evaluate the adaptive strategies: (i) Portfolio Analysis; and (ii) Strategic Position and Action Evaluation (SPACE) Analysis.

Portfolio Analysis

Portfolio analysis, popularized by the Boston Consulting Group (BCG), has become a fundamental tool for strategic analysis. The market position of the health care organization as a whole or its separate programmes can be examined in terms of its share of the market and the rate of the industry's growth (Robin et al., 1983). As illustrated in the Figure 5.1 the portfolio analysis matrix graphically portrays the differences among the various metaphorical categories of personnel (Stars, Cash Cows, Problem Children, and Dogs) in terms of concern and competence for quality of health care.

To achieve the desired output, we have to enhance the concern and competence of the key personnel in the system, i.e., district level officers, medical officer in-charges, and auxiliary nurse mid-wives. By using the concept of portfolio analysis, in terms of their concern for quality of care and competency for providing quality of care, we will able to obtain the adaptive strategy for these key personnel.

Figure 5.3

Portfolio Analysis for Quality of Health Care

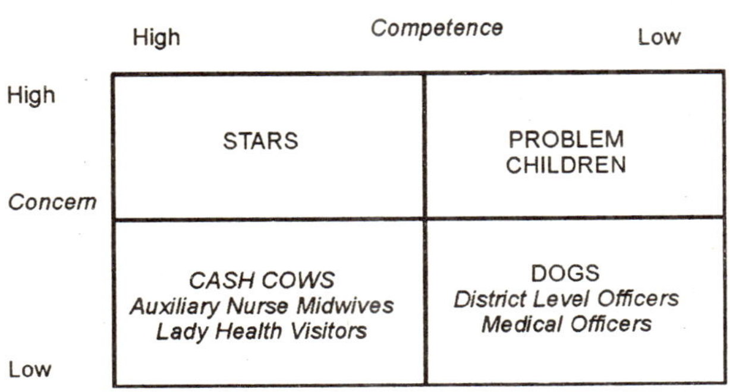

Stars: The category of human resources that fall in this quadrant (high concern and high competency) represent the organization's best long-run opportunity for achieving quality of health care. These personnel have high competence and concern for quality of health care. These key personnel should be provided resources. In our example of Udaipur district, the analysis from system's diagnosis shows that no category of personnel falls in this quadrant.

Cash Cows: The key personnel in this quadrant have low concern for quality of health care but have high competence for providing quality of health care. In our example of Udaipur district, the lady health visitors (LHVs) and auxiliary nurse midwives (ANMs) fall in this quadrant. The position of lady health visitor is a promotional one. They are promoted from auxiliary nurse midwives with five years of experience. They are trained in IUD insertion, and conduct antenatal care examination and deliveries. Lady health visitors are found to have acquired technical as well as behavioural competencies to provide the quality of health care. However, they are found to have a low degree of concern. They are supervisors for auxiliary nurse midwives. The low concern for quality of health care may be reflected in the fact that they are supposed to conduct monitoring visits to the working areas to assess the performance of the auxiliary nurse midwives, and explain the technical points in providing clinical services, but, it was found during the discussions with district level officers, that they do the monthly monitoring but it is not focused on the quality of services. It was also found that they generally do not review and analyse the client records on quality of care issues. Rather, they focus on the number of acceptors.

As for the Information, Education and Communication (IEC) plan, every month lady health visitors are expected to visit at least 15 villages with low couple protection rate or high infant mortality and maternal mortality rate auxiliary nurse midwives, carry out activities to inform and educate the community regarding reproductive health services. But it was observed that these monitoring visits are not being undertaken regularly in the district, which reflects their low level of concern for the quality of services.

The auxiliary nurse midwives fall in this quadrant. They are grassroots level workers in the health care delivery system, and have direct contact with the clients. They generally live in a village setting and know the local language, so that it facilitates them in maintaining the interpersonal relations with the clients The concern of auxiliary nurse midwives for quality of care may be reflected in the elements of the quality of care framework: choice of method and information given to clients. The concurrent evaluation revealed that in the district only 57 per cent of the clients were given a method choice at the time of adopting the family planning method. This shows the auxiliary nurse midwives' concern about their clients, even though it is not forced from above. The auxiliary nurse midwives are also concerned about the continuity and follow-up mechanism of the services. The concurrent evaluation revealed that about 49 per cent of the current users of spacing methods received a follow-up visit by auxiliary nurse midwives within a month after adoption of the method, and about 79 per cent of the sterilization clients received a follow-up visit after the adoption of the method. The concern is found to be medium in case of maternal health services, where it was found that only 12 per cent of the women received at least three visits during their antenatal period, and about 27 per cent received a follow-up visit by the auxiliary nurse midwives during the postnatal period within a week after delivery. Only 5 per cent of the clients were told about possible side effects; 2 per cent were told about both the advantages and the disadvantages of the method; only 12 per cent were advised about periodical check-ups; and only 8 per cent were advised on proper breast-feeding. This shows the low level of concern for providing quality services. Table 3.1 reveals that in the district only 16 per cent of the spacing method users were told about regular follow-up visits and only 1 per cent were told to report to the health worker in case of any side effects.

The data used to assess the competence of auxiliary nurse midwives is based on whether the provider offered services that are expected as part of a competent service (as defined by an obstetrician/gynecologist, rather than by the actual quality of the services provided). In terms of measures of technical competence in case of family planning services, whether the provider inquired about the clients' health problems and menstruation status at the time of adoption, and whether the necessary examinations were performed by the provider or not, are taken into account. Table 3.1 shows that only 36 per cent of the clients were inquired about their general health problems, and 22 per cent were inquired about their menstruation cycle before providing the method. Moreover, 21 per cent clients reported that blood pressure was recorded by the worker at the time of adopting the family planning method, and 22 per cent clients reported that vaginal and breast examinations were performed by the health worker at the time of adopting the family planning method.

The technical competence of the auxiliary nurse midwives, in case of maternal health services, is assessed on the various things the worker is expected to do for a pregnant woman for better care. These include: (i) taking medical history (obstetric history, general health, weight and height, calculating expected date of delivery, and assessing risk factors); (ii) examination (general, physical, obstetric and edema); and (iii) inquiring about bleeding/pain in abdomen. Table 3.1indicates that only 3 per cent of women reported that obstetric history was noted, only 5 per cent reported that general health problems were enquired about, about 42 per cent reported that their weight and height were recorded, about 40 per cent said that the expected date of delivery was worked out, and 40 per cent reported that risk factors were assessed for them during the antenatal period. Moreover, 57 per cent of the women reported about general physical examination, 8 per cent about obstetric examination, and 61 per cent about edema examination having been done by the health worker during the antenatal period. About 68 per cent of the women reported that they were inquired about bleeding/pain in abdomen during the antenatal period.

Problem Children: Problem children have low competence, yet have a high level of concern for quality of care. The analysis from system's diagnosis found that no category of personnel falls in this quadrant.

Dogs: These personnel have low concern for quality of care and low competence for providing quality services. The district level officers and medical officers fall in this quadrant. These key processors have low degree of competence for managing quality of health care, and also low level of concern.

The district level personnel require certain competencies, i.e., technical and behavioural, for providing quality services. The district level processor should be competent to manage the various aspects of competence, i.e., competence of the clinical technique of providers, the observance of protocols, and meticulous asepsis required to provide clinical family planning methods and safe motherhood services. During the discussions with district level officials, it was revealed that they did not practice any method to manage the above competencies, i.e., they were not competent to manage the quality of care in the district. However, due to concurrent evaluation, they showed some concern about the quality of care.

The medical officers also fall in this quadrant. The low concern of medical officers for quality of care is reflected in the fact that, many a time, the primary health centre medical officers working in remote areas visit primary health centres only after a long interval to get their salary. The general attitude of the doctors is that they are employed as servants of the government, and are responsible for serving their supervisors rather than the clients' needs. The medical officer tries to keep his supervisor happy, rather than supporting his subordinates in their functions to serve the clients' needs. Practically, this translates into neglect of the clients, compromise on safety standards in performing procedures, and at times, work is done only on paper. The medical officer never discusses quality of care in the primary health centre meeting, reflecting his low level of concern for quality services. They discuss only targets and achievements.

In case of infrastructure problems, there are not only problems of civil engineering and physical maintenance, but also problems of attitude, habits, and behaviour, which reflect their poor concern for quality of care. This does not require much additional resources. However, it requires the concern of the staff for quality. There are instances of excellent maintenance when the medical officer in-charge in particular has taken keen interest in it. Hence, lack of both systematic management as well as individual initiative contributes to poor infrastructure facilities in the primary health centre.

From the above discussion, it is clear that to achieve the desired output, we have to

- Convert the cash cows (auxiliary nurse midwives and lady health visitors) to stars by improving their concern for quality of care through training, public performance rating system, and dual record system;

- Convert the dogs (district level officers and medical officers working at community health centres and primary health centres) to stars by improving their concern and competence for quality of care through training on various aspects of quality assurance.

Strategic Position and Action Evaluation (SPACE) Analysis

Strategic position and action evaluation (SPACE), an extension of the two-dimensional portfolio analysis, is used to determine the appropriate strategic posture of the organization. By using SPACE, the health manager can incorporate a number of factors into the analysis and examine a particular strategic alternative from several perspectives (Rowe et al.,1989).

SPACE analysis suggests the appropriateness of strategic alternatives based on factors relating to four dimensions: industry strength, environmental stability, the organization's competitive advantage, and the organization's financial strength. The SPACE chart is shown in Figure 5.4.

Figure 5.4

Strategic Position and Action Evaluation (SPACE) Chart

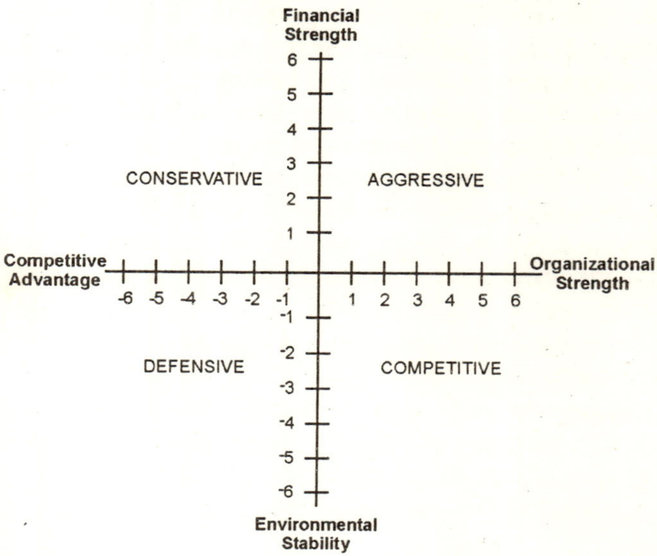

The definitions of the four quadrants of the SPACE chart are given below (Alan et al., 1989):

Aggressive Posture: This posture is typical in an attractive industry with little environmental turbulence. The organization enjoys a definite competitive advantage, which it can protect with financial strength. The critical factor is the entry of new competitors. Organizations in this situation should take full advantage of opportunities, look for acquisition candidates in their own or related areas, increase market share, and concentrate resources on products having a definite competitive edge.

Competitive Posture: This posture is typical in an attractive industry. The organization enjoys a competitive advantage in a relatively unstable environment. The critical factor is financial strength. Organizations in this situation should acquire financial resources to increase marketing thrust, add to the sales force, extend or improve the product line, invest in productivity, reduce costs, protect competitive advantage in a declining market, and attempt to merge with a cash-rich organization.

Conservative Posture: This posture is typical in a stable market with low growth. Here, the organization focuses on financial stability. The critical factor is product competitiveness. Organizations in this situation should prune the product line, reduce costs, focus on improving cash flow, protect competitive products, develop new products, and gain into more attractive markets.

Defensive Posture: This posture is typical of an unattractive industry in which the organization lacks a competitive product and financial strength. The critical factor is competitiveness. Firms in this situation should prepare to retreat from the market, discontinue marginally profitable products, aggressively reduce costs, cut capacity, and defer or minimise investments.

Listed under each of the dimensions are factors to which individual numerical values, ranging from 0 to 6, can be assigned. The numbers are then added together and divided by the number of factors to yield an average. The averages for environmental stability and competitive advantage each have the number six subtracted from them to produce a negative number. The average for each dimension is then plotted on the appropriate axis of the SPACE chart and connected to create a four-sided polygon. Factor scales for each of the dimensions, e.g., industry strength (IS), environmental stability (ES), competitive advantage (CA), and financial strength (FS) of the quality of care of reproductive health services in the district are presented in Tables 5.3a–5.3d. The values for the factors listed under each of the dimensions are determined by the results of system's diagnosis. The resulting shape of the polygon can be used to identify four strategic postures – aggressive, competitive, conservative, and defensive. The quadrant with the largest area is suggested as the most appropriate general strategic position.

Table 5.3a

SPACE Analysis on Quality of Health Care: Factors Determining Environmental Stability

Factors Determining Environmental Stability (ES)			
Technological changes	Many	0 1 2 **3** 4 5 6	Few
Demand for quality services	Many	0 1 2 **3** 4 5 6	Few
Socio-economic status of population	Low	0 1 **2** 3 4 5 6	High
Transport development	Weak	0 1 **2** 3 4 5 6	Strong
Communication development	Weak	0 1 **2** 3 4 5 6	Strong
State government support	Low	0 1 2 3 4 **5** 6	High
Role of NGOs and PMPs	Low	0 1 **2** 3 4 5 6	High
Regulation for PMPs for quality services	Weak	0 **1** 2 3 4 5 6	Strong
Average – 6 = 2.5 – 6 = –3.5			

Critical Factors: Regulation for PMPs, Role of NGOs in delivering quality of care, transport and communication development.

Table 5.3b

SPACE Analysis on Quality of Health Care: Factors Determining Organizational Strength

Factors Determining Organizational Strength (OS)			
Growth potential	Many	0 1 2 **3** 4 5 6	Few
Financial stability	Many	0 1 2 **3** 4 5 6	Few
Doctors at PHC/CHC	Inadequate	0 1 2 **3** 4 5 6	Adequate
Manpower at SC level	Inadequate	0 1 2 3 4 **5** 6	Adequate
Physical infrastructure (buildings)	Poor	0 1 2 3 4 **5** 6	Good
Basic amenities at facilities	Poor	0 1 **2** 3 4 5 6	Good
Staff concern for quality	Weak	0 1 **2** 3 4 5 6	Strong
Staff competence for quality of care	Low	0 1 **2** 3 4 5 6	High
Monitoring	Low	0 1 **2** 3 4 5 6	High
Staff motivation	Weak	0 **1** 2 3 4 5 6	Strong
Average = 2.8			

Critical Factors: Inadequate number of doctors, adequate ANMs, low level of concern for quality, low level of competence of staff for quality services, weak staff motivation for quality of care.

Table 5.3c

SPACE Analysis on Quality of Health Care: Factors Determining Competitive Advantage

Factors Determining Competitive Advantage (CA)			
Market share	Small	0 1 2 3 **4** 5 6	High
Quality of service	Poor	0 1 **2** 3 4 5 6	Few
Experienced field staff	Less	0 1 2 3 4 **5** 6	More
Customer loyalty	Low	0 1 **2** 3 4 5 6	High
Technological know-how	Simple	0 1 2 **3** 4 5 6	Complex
Vertical integration	Low	0 1 2 3 4 **5** 6	High
Average –6 = 3.5 – 6 = –2.5			

Critical Factors: Low quality of services, experienced field staff, high vertical integration.

Table 5.3d

SPACE Analysis on Quality of Health Care: Factors Determining Financial Strength

Factors Determining Financial Strength (FS)			
Separate budget for quality assurance	Low	**0** 1 2 3 4 5 6	High
Stability of operating cost	Low	0 1 **2** 3 4 5 6	High
Overall economic status of population	Low	0 1 **2** 3 4 5 6	High
Integration with other programmes	Low	0 1 2 **3** 4 5 6	High
Dependency on donor for financial resources	Low	**0** 1 2 3 4 5 6	High
Average = 1.4			

Critical Factors: Inadequate budget for quality assurance, low dependency on donors

Which of the adaptive strategic alternatives is most appropriate for the quality of reproductive health care services in the study district? The dimensions for this system are plotted on the SPACE matrix shown in Tables 5.3a–5.3d.

The analysis demonstrates that the organization is competing fairly well in an unstable but attractive organization segment. This organization cannot be too aggressive because it has few financial resources and the environment is a bit unstable. Therefore, it should adopt a competitive posture. It is important to understand that the SPACE chart is a summary display. Each factor should be analysed individually as well. In particular, factors with very high or very low scores should receive special attention. Figure 5.5 shows the adaptive alternatives for each strategic posture.

From the above analysis, using system diagnosis, portfolio analysis and SPACE analysis, it can be concluded that the guiding strategy for the present system has been to establish a sound desired output for quality of care of reproductive health services assuming the project period is three years. To achieve this strategy, we had set a sound desired output for quality of care, which is as follows: "To achieve the quality of care at the level of 50 (overall score of quality-of-care) by the end of the project."

To achieve the above-mentioned desired output, efforts are needed to improve those factors which affect the quality most. It has been seen that improving the key human resources will have the most effect. Therefore, the concern for quality and competence of the service provider to provide the quality services has to be enhanced by adopting a competitive posture. It will be enhanced through capacity building of processors working at district, community health centres, primary health centres and sub-centres level for improving quality of reproductive health services. The quality improvement programme has to initiate in the district keeping in view the current level of quality of reproductive health services. Apart from capacity building efforts, efforts are also required to institutionalizing *"risk-reward system"* through public performance rating system and dual record system.

Figure 5.5

SPACE Profile for Quality of Health Care

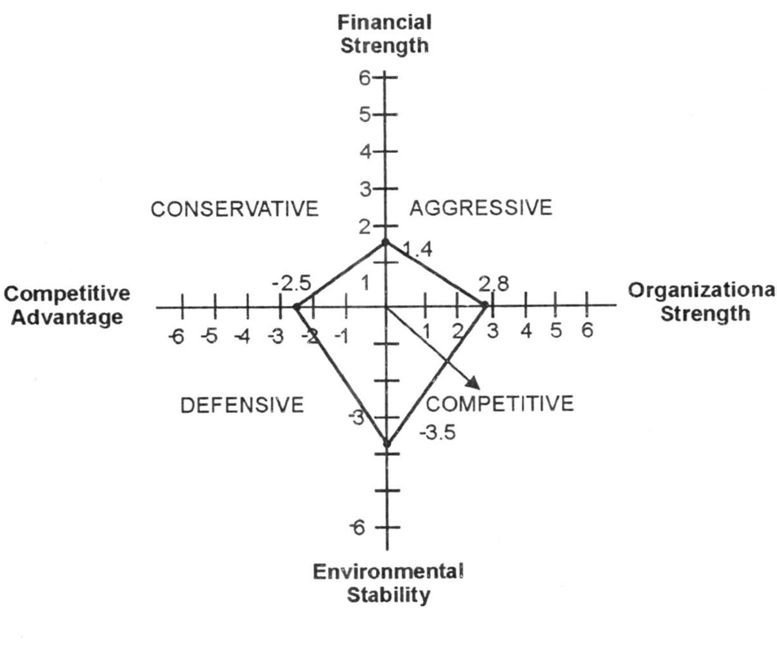

CHAPTER 6

Implementing Quality of Health Care

Strategic implementation is the process of translating the strategy into specific programmes. Therefore, in the implementation stage, employees and managers are mobilized to translate formulated strategy into action. It is in the implementation stage that managing human, financial, informational, and physical resources becomes most important. During this stage, the strategy is accomplished (Duncan et al., 1995).

The guiding strategy, for the present system, has been to establish a sound desired output for quality of care of reproductive health services in the district. To achieve this strategy, we had proposed a sound desired output for quality of care, which is as follows: "To achieve the quality of care at the level of 50 (overall score of quality-of-care) by the end of the project." To achieve the above-mentioned desired output, we have to improve those factors, which affect the quality most. It has been seen that improving the key human resources will have the most effect. Therefore, the concern for quality and competence of the service provider to provide the quality services has to be enhanced. It will be enhanced through the following activities: (1) training and capacity building programme; and (2) risk and reward system. The training and capacity building programme will involve the following activities: quality leadership training, training of trainer, counselling skills training, and technical skills training. The risk and reward system will include the following activities: public performance rating system, and dual record system.

The strategy will be implemented in a phased manner. The district will be the main planning and implementing unit. It will be implemented as an integral part of the existing public health system.

Strategic Assumptions

The strategy is based on a number of important assumptions:

Ownership: Quality improvement teams will be more committed to implementing plans if they are helped to analyse and tackle problems that they themselves perceive to be important. The quality improvement process does not supply ready-made solutions to problems identified.

Teamwork: Problems are identified and solutions developed by the members of the quality improvement team. Responsibility for implementation is shared because tasks are assigned to different team members and not just to the medical officer in charge.

Repetition: Repetition management and planning skills improve with practice and guidance. The quality improvement process allows district health officers to review progress after a relatively short period (3–7 months) so that adjustments can be made in the light of experience. The series of workshops ensures that reviews take place at regular intervals.

Incremental Learning: The workshops are structured to allow teams to build on initial achievements. New ideas are introduced as they become relevant. As quality improvement teams gain experience, they gradually develop and implement more sophisticated plans.

Government Support: Policy level support will be available for improving of quality of care of reproductive health services. It is accepted that the most important things happen not at the workshops but between them. Support and encouragement to district health teams and other teams between workshops are thus an indispensable part of the process. Facility Support Equipment, drugs, accessories and facilities for appropriate level of care will be assured at community health centre, primary health centre and sub-centre levels.

Staff Availability: Staff will be made available according to the sanctioned posts at the various levels of the health care delivery system and it will be assured that the key processors will not be transferred during project implementation.

Translating Strategy into Action

In a well-conceived strategic or operating plan, the changes required of an operating system to implement a particular strategy are outline in the form of a sequence of tasks and sub-task. Each task specifies the time framefor completing the task, the resources needed to complete the task, and cost.

To transfer a strategy into plan of action, the following steps are followed:

- Tasks to be completed
- Time frame
- Persons responsible
- Resources needed
- Costs

Tasks to be Completed: Once the objectives have been established, the next step is to list the tasks necessary to meet the objectives. After listing the major tasks, sub-tasks are identified to complete that major task, which is followed by sequencing them (Table 6.1).

Table 6.1

Identification of Tasks and Sub-tasks for Implementation of Strategy

Tasks	*Sub-tasks*
Setting the Stage for Quality Improvement	Organize for institutionalizing quality
	Assess organization culture, employee attitudes, and customer perceptions
	Analyse COPQ
	Define quality of care framework

Cont'd ...

Cont'd ...

Training for Quality Improvement	Organize a workshop to sensitise state and district officials about quality of care
	Organize training workshops for district officials and medical officers
	Organize quality leadership training for team leaders
	Organize training of trainers for quality improvement
	Organize counselling skill training for nursing staff
	Organize technical skill training for nursing staff
	Quality orientation programme for private medical practitioners
	Refresher training for medical and nursing staff
Dual Record System	Organize workshop for designing client-based card
	Launch client-based card system in pilot PHC
	Feedback and corrective action on client-based card system
	Introduce modified client-based record system in the district
Performance Rating System	Organize workshop for designing public rating system
	Launch rating system in pilot PHC
	Feedback and corrective action
	Introduce modified rating system in the district
Monitoring and Control	Organize bi-annual meeting of quality council
	Organize monthly meeting of district quality council
	Continuous meeting/review by quality teams at CHC, PHC and SC level
	Conduct mid-term evaluation
	Conduct end-of-project evaluation

Time frame: It is useful to put a start date and an end date for each task. That allows us to build a calendar of activities. Here, we are giving an estimated time frame in weeks for completing the particular activity. A schedule is a route map for making a journey through the future. The implementation schedule informs us of what events should occur at specific future times if our implementation objective is to be attained. Scheduling is critical to making the project successful. Figure 6.1 shows the quality improvement milestone chart describing tasks to be implemented along with time line.

Figure 6.1

Quality Improvement Milestone Chart

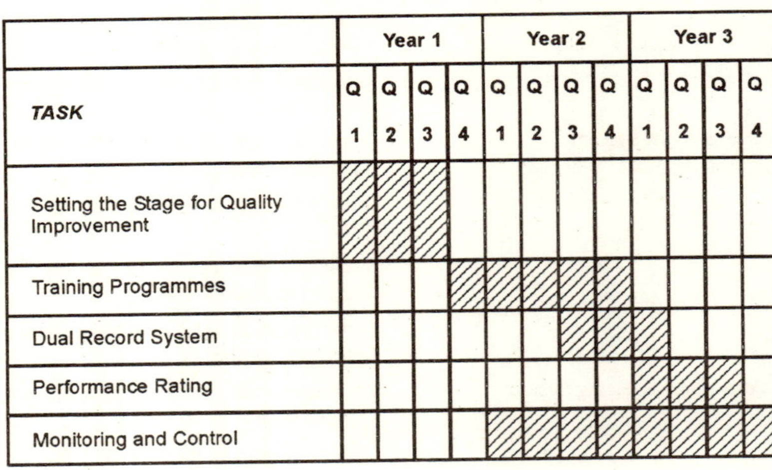

Table 6.2

Action Plan for Implementing Quality Improvement Strategy

Task	*Sub-task*	*Expected Outcome*	*Time frame (Weeks)*	*Persons Responsible*
Setting the Stage for Quality Improvement	Organizing for quality	Quality council, design team, lead team, and quality improvement teams formulated	2	CMHO

Cont'd ...

Cont'd ...

	Analysing COPQ	Cost of poor quality (COPQ) estimated	2	CMHO
	Assessing Organization Culture	Organizational culture assessed	2	MCHO
	Setting Quality of Care Framework	Quality of health care framework for the district finalized	1	Deputy CMHO (Family Welfare)
Training Programmes	Organizing Sensitization Seminar	30 district level officials sensitized on quality of health care	1	CMHO
	Training Workshops	175 health professionals participated in the workshop and exposed on quality of health care (including district officials, junior specialists, senior medical officers, medical officers	4	CMHO
	Quality Leadership Training	100 health professionals trained in leadership for quality improvement	8	MCH Officer
	Training of Trainers for Quality Improvement	60 health professionals trained as trainer for providing quality improvement training	3	MCH Officer
	Counselling Skill Training	600 nursing staff trained in interpersonal communication skills	10	Deputy CMHO (Family Welfare)

Cont'd ...

Cont'd ...

	Technical Skill Training	600 nursing staff trained in technical skills	10	Deputy CMHO (Family Welfare)
	Orientation Training for Private Medical Practitioners	60 private medical practitioners exposed to quality of care concepts and framework	2	Deputy CMHO (Family Welfare)
	Refresher Training for Medical and Nursing Staff	Medical officers and nursing staff	10	Deputy CMHO (Family Welfare)
Dual Record System	Designing Workshop	Dual record system designed and guidelines developed	2	CMHO
	Launching in Pilot PHC	Dual record system launched in on pilot basis	2	Deputy CMHO (Family Welfare)
	Taking Corrective Actions	Corrective actions and modifications done	2	Deputy CMHO (Family Welfare)
	Launching in Complete District	Dual record system launched in complete district	4	Deputy CMHO (Family Welfare)
Performance Rating	Designing Workshop	Rating system designed for sub-centre service quality	2	CMHO
	Launching in Pilot PHC	Performance rating system launched in pilot area	2	Deputy CMHO (Family Welfare)
	Taking Corrective Actions	Corrective actions and modifications done	2	Deputy CMHO (Family Welfare)

Cont'd ...

Cont'd ...

	Launching in the complete district	Performance rating system launched in complete District	4	CMHO
	Training of ANM/LHV	600 ANM/LHV trained in dual record system and performance rating system	10	Deputy CMHO (Family Welfare)
Monitoring and Control	Reviewing by Quality Improvement Teams	Monthly reviews done by quality improvement teams	Continuous	Team Leaders
	Conducting Annual Reviews	Gaps identified through annual reviews for further modifications	2 per year	CMHO/ Quality Council
	Conducting End-line Evaluation	End-line evaluation completed and Project Completion Report Prepared	10	CMHO/ Quality Council

Person Responsible: Who will be responsible for the particular task? We have to decide who will take lead. What is important is that each task is assigned to a specific person.

Resources Needed: Resource included both material and human. The human resource means the type of people, i.e., trainees, trainers, staff, consultant, etc. who will be involved in carrying out the task. Material resources are the items that will be needed to get the task done. This may be project document, training modules, training materials, room, official letter, stationary, etc. If the resources are not readily available in the system, they will have to be generated from outside the system by generating funds from the donor agency, and in some cases, from community financing. The resources required for implementing the strategy, and their availability in the system have been shown in Table 6.3.

Table 6.3

Resources Requirement Matrix for Implementation of Strategy for Improving Quality of Care

Task/Sub-tasks	*Resources Needed*	*Resources Available in the System*	*Resources to be Generated*
Organizing for Quality	Top management support	Yes	
	Official support	Yes	
	Support at CHC/PHC	Yes	
	Official letter	No	To be issued
Analysing COPQ	Request from design team	No	To be done
	Approval from QC	No	To get approval
	Consultant	No	To be hired
	Support of design team	Yes	
	Support of district officials	Yes	
	Budget documents	Yes	
	Accounts	Yes	
	Staff support	Yes	
Assessing Organization Culture	Consultant	No	To be hired
	Design team support	Yes	
	Support from district level	Yes	
	Staff time	Yes	
Setting Quality of Care Framework	Literature review	No	Visit IIHMR
	Consultant	No	To be hired
	Design team support	Yes	

Cont'd …

Cont'd ...

Organizing Sensitization Seminar	Official letter	No	To be issued
	Administrative support	Yes	
	List of participants	No	To be prepared
	Seminar arrangements	No	To be made
	Study findings	Yes	
	Project documents	Yes	
Training Workshops	Official letter	No	To be issued
	Administrative support	Yes	
	List of participants	No	To be prepared
	Seminar arrangements	No	To be made
	Study findings	Yes	
	Project documents	Yes	
Quality Leadership Training	Official letter	No	To be issued
	Administrative support	Yes	
	List of participants	No	To be prepared
	Seminar arrangements	No	To be made
	Study findings	Yes	
	Project documents	Yes	
TOT for Quality Improvement	Official letter	No	To be issued
	Administrative support	Yes	
	Curriculum content	No	To be prepared

Cont'd ...

Cont'd ...

	List of participants	No	To be made
	Training material	No	To be developed
	Training arrangements	No	To be made
	Study findings	Yes	
	Project documents	Yes	
Counselling Skill Training	Official letter	No	To be issued
	Administrative support	Yes	
	List of participants	No	To be prepared
	Training arrangements	No	To be made
	Study findings	Yes	
	Project documents	Yes	
Technical Skill Training	Official letter	No	To be issued
	Administrative support	Yes	
	List of participants	No	To be prepared
	Seminar arrangements	No	To be made
	Study findings	Yes	
	Project documents	Yes	
Refresher Training	Workers QI experience	Yes	
	Administrative support	Yes	
	List of participants	No	To be prepared
	Training arrangements	No	To be made
	PHC/SC data	Yes	

Cont'd ...

Cont'd ...

	Room	Yes	
Designing Workshop for dual record system	Official letter	No	To be issued
	Administrative support	Yes	
	List of participants	No	To be prepared
	Workshop arrangements	No	To be made
	Samples of cards	No	To be collected
	Consultant/facilitator	No	To be hired
Launching in Pilot PHC	Support of PHC staff	Yes	
	Cards	No	To be printed
	Clients	Yes	
Taking Corrective Actions	QI Team	Yes	
	Experience of workers	No	To be documented
Launching in the District	Official letter	No	To be made
	Support of staff	Yes	Yes
	Printing of cards	No	To be printed
	Distribution of cards	No	To be distributed
	Transportation	Yes	
Designing Workshop for performance rating	Official letter	No	To be issued
	Administrative support	Yes	
	List of participants	No	To be prepared
	Workshop arrangements	No	To be made

Cont'd ...

Cont'd ...

	Samples of cards	No	To be collected
	Consultant/facilitator	No	To be hired
Launching in Pilot PHC	Support of PHC staff	Yes	
	Guidelines	No	
	Clients awareness	No	To be made
Taking Corrective Action	QI Team	Yes	
	Experience of workers	No	To be documented
	Experience of clients	No	To be discussed
Launching in the district	Official letter	No	To be made
	Support of staff	Yes	Yes
	Printing of cards	No	To be printed
	Distribution of cards	No	To be distributed
	Transportation	Yes	
Monitoring and control	Supervision plan	No	To be developed
	Supervisory check-list	No	To be developed
	Manpower	Yes	
	Client card for follow-up	Yes	
	Service statistics	Yes	
	QOC guidelines	Yes	
	Rating system guidelines	Yes	
	Evaluation guidelines	No	To be developed

Costs: The implementation plan has the aim of maximizing the existing resources. Based on the resources required, we have to estimate the detailed costs of implementing the quality improvement at the district level.

Setting the Stage for Quality Improvement

Establishing an effective quality improvement process and culture in the organization is a sizable undertaking. Considerable preparation is required to do it well and to ensure its lasting effect. As with any other investment, establishing a quality process requires up-front effort and a financial outlay. It also requires a firm resolve or commitment to see it through. Often, this commitment is more difficult to attain than the fund needed to get started. Commitment is also more important than fund. Without strong backing and passionate leadership, the monetary investment will be squandered since the effort will surely fail. Strong commitment will ensure that you realize an attractive return on the investment made. The following sub-tasks will be carried out for setting the stage for an effective quality improvement process and culture: (a) organizing for quality improvement; (b) assessing corporate culture, employee attitudes and client perceptions about quality of care; (c) analysing the cost of poor quality (COPQ), and (d) defining quality of care framework.

Organizing for Quality Improvement

The first step in organizing for quality requires the formation in three phases of a simple and mostly parallel organizational structure as illustrated in figure below. These structures begin to define the flow of responsibility for the key quality architects and developers, as well as define the hierarchy of support.

Phase I quality organization should be established quietly and without fanfare once senior management has developed enough interest in quality to warrant a more serious examination of how the concepts may be applied to their particular organization.

Figure 6.2

Organizational Structure for Quality Improvement

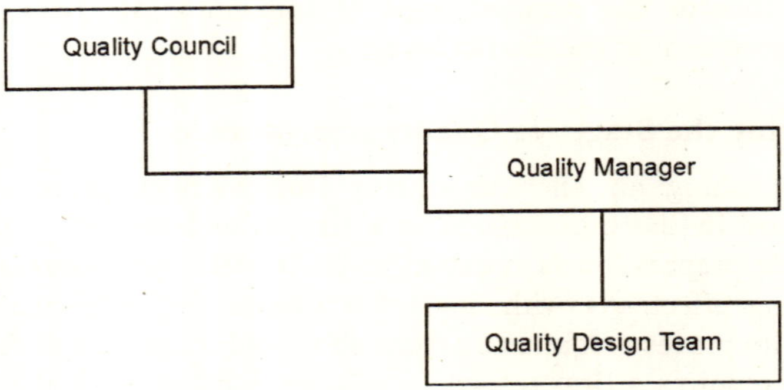

Quality Council: A quality council will be formed. The council will be the top-level steering group that will make the key decisions and authorize the support needed to plan, study, design, implement, and nurture the process. The council will be chaired by the director (family welfare) and include the other senior executives or officers who report to him or her. The council should not be viewed as a body separate and distinct from the existing top management group. It is the existing top management group, the one reporting, for example, to the board of directors. It should be borne in mind that we are not building another structure; we are creating a parallel structure. Quality council business should be conducted whenever the top managers meet to pursue other matters. That is, council business should be a major new and ever-present agenda item for the regular staff meeting.

Council members, both individually and collectively, will commit themselves from day one not only to support quality of care, but also to involve themselves personally with the quality process so that it will be successfully implemented. This hands-on, top-level involvement is the most critical factor in the successful development and implementation of quality of care.

The quality council's first meeting should be devoted to developing a mission statement a list of key responsibilities the council reserves for itself for the development, implementation, and ongoing administration of quality of care. A sample of quality council mission statement is illustrated below:

Figure 6.3
A Quality Council Mission Statement

Quality Council Mission Statement

Mission Summary

The Quality Council of Health Department of district will direct, support and participate in the development and administration of quality of reproductive health services in the district. The council will ensure that key decisions regarding quality of care are made and that the financial and human resources needed are made available.

Specific Responsibilities

1. To formulate, communicate, promote, and guide the quality improvement process.
2. To ensure that organization reward and reorganization systems support and reinforce quality improvement participation and success.
3. To approve quality project proposals to be pursued by quality improvement teams.
4. To monitor and communicate results achieved through the quality improvement process.
5. To lead the quality planning process.
6. To participate in recognition of events that celebrates quality success.
7. To provide the financial and human resources needed to effectively pursue quality improvement process.
8. To ensure that adequate training is provided in quality assurance and quality improvement in order to establish an environment of continuous learning.
9. To ensure top management's personal and direct involvement in the project activities.

Design Team: After establishing the Quality Council, it will be necessary to appoint a Quality Manager who will recruit a Quality Design Team from within the organization at district level. The quality manager should be a respected executive currently holding a senior-level position at the district level. He should also be appointed to the quality council.

The selection of the quality manager is very important. The "right" person must be chosen. He would be one of the best executives. The right candidate is someone you really don't want to choose because that person is seen as critical to his current function. The right person has an excellent reputation within the organization with an outstanding track record. He must be an excellent communicator and a tireless contributor. Finally, the right choice will be someone who has demonstrated the ability to manage large projects and who has a strong interest in quality improvement and customer satisfaction.

Once a choice is made, the quality manager will recruit the design team. The design team will include six to eight highly respected middle-level managers (senior medical officers/medical officers) or other key people selected from a variety of units within the organization. Like the quality manager, candidates for the design team should possess leadership skills, be excellent communicators, and so on. They must also have the explicit support of their respective bosses for participating on the team because some backup for them may be needed for their regular job. Collectively, they should form a compatible group – a cohesive team.

The design team is extremely important, for the obvious reason that it will make a recommendation to top management on a matter of great, long-range significance. It is also very important for a more subtle reason. By far, people in many organization with whom I have discussed the idea of establishing a corporate quality process have had great difficulty in winning middle-management support. Once the top management is committed, most people at the lower levels embrace the quality movement quickly and enthusiastically. The middle levels, however, often feel ignored or threatened. One way to help avoid this is to set up a middle-level design team. Team members will have ideas about how to include the middle levels and their rising enthusiasm will be transmitted to their peers. As a result, down the road, we will have an easier time establishing a true, organization-wide commitment to quality and we certainly need middle management's support and involvement to make it happen.

The first activity for the design team will be a two-day off-site meeting. The quality council should be present only for the first few hours to review its own mission and the mission of the design team. The rest of the day should be devoted to a short seminar on complex-change management provided by an outside consultant. The consultant will focus on some team-building activities during the day. Informal socializing would occur at dinner, and more team building to take place. The second day, with some help from the consultant, should be spent planning how the team will pursue the first part of its mission: studying quality of care.

Because the first part of the mission requires a thorough study of quality of care, the team may consider study findings, available books on quality of care, seminars, and the use of a quality improvement consultant. Team members need to understand the broad concepts and a variety of approaches so that they can design a quality improvement process that fits their own culture and circumstances.

Before adjourning from the two-day meeting, the members of the team should decide when they will meet next and how frequently future meanings will occur. Then, to get on with it, and keep the quality council advised along the way.

We have now reached a critical point in our quality improvement journey. Top management, in the form of the quality council, has accepted the design team's recommendation to develop and test a Quality of Care Framework. This design and testing phase will take several months, perhaps as long as a year or more, depending on the size of the company, the resources made available, the competition for time and resources within the company, the skill of the design team, and a number of other related factors.

However, at this point, it is time to add two more elements to phase I quality organization structure. First, each major component of reproductive health services, i.e., family planning and safe motherhood should form its own quality council or quality lead team and should set a mission similar to that adopted by the top-level quality council. The senior officer should chair the lead team of that service (family planning and safe motherhood) or major service unit (community health centre), and it should consist of those who would report to the executive. A lead team for family planning services and safe motherhood services should be chaired by a person with high level of competence and concern for quality of care. The primary objective of a lead team is to ensure that quality improvement effectively implemented and utilized within its area of responsibility. An important point to be made here is that the lead teams are to feel a strong sense of ownership for quality of care within their respective areas.

Second, a suitable community health centre and/or primary health centre should be chosen as a pilot test site. It is within this test unit that the quality improvement process (like quality of care framework, dual record system, and performance rating system), when it is initially designed, will be plugged in for a trial run. Quality teams will be established at community health centre, primary health centre and sub-centre level as an effort to improve the quality of the work performed through teamwork and participation by all staff. Staff at all levels will be included in an effort to tap creativity and innovation throughout the organization. Quality teams will be used to solve many day-to-day problems or those that cause customer dissatisfaction. The quality teams activities will be completely decentralized. Each institution or service facility will have its own quality teams. The quality team may arise from a need to solve a specific problem or be on-going. An annual convention of quality teams will be held (Quality Day) and awards will be presented to those teams which perform outstanding work.

Assessing Organization Culture

A climate survey will be conducted using a firm that specializes in conducting such surveys, for assessing the internal human relations environment and measuring customer attitudes. The result will be carefully analysed and shared with the employees. A group of people should be formed to help develop ideas for improvement, based on the survey results. This employee involvement sends a signal that is compatible with the quality improvement concepts of involvement and idea generation. Various tools may be used to generate ideas, i.e., brainstorming, affinity diagram, etc.

The climate survey should consist of two parts. One would measure attitudes relating to work life and conditions such as supervision, appraisal, rewards, concern for quality, and communications. The other part to assess the organization culture. The organization, through its day-to-day actions and priorities, will sends signals that define what it thinks is important and proper. Employees should then behave according to their interpretation of these signals. For example, the reward system may recognize people who have performed a large number of sterilizations, but virtually ignore the quality of what has been performed.

An assessment of organizational culture will help determine changes in organization programmes and management behaviour that are necessary to support a quality improvement process. The general purpose of the survey is to help ensure that the employee population is ready and willing to participate in building a total quality culture, an attitude based on trust, teamwork, objective problem-solving, and enhanced accountability.

The climate survey will help assess both internal and external customers' perceptions about quality of care. It will help to assess how employees feel about the support received from the internal clients' needs. People usually have a good idea as to how external customers feel about their services. They will make a list for prioritizing them.

Analysing the Cost of Poor Quality (COPQ)

COPQ, the cost of not doing things right the first time can amount to a sizeable sum. A short study is to be conducted to determine at least a ballpark figure for COPQ. A short study, because it is difficult and unnecessary to be precise. Good estimates should provide the data that attract top management's attention. The Quality Council, upon the recommendation of the design team, would commission a group of three to four people from the health economics and financing area to study the COPQ over a period of time. The investigation will include interviews with the key processors and other people in the system. These interviews should be strictly confidential in order to have useful data.

Developing an estimate of the COPQ can be helpful in gaining top management's commitment to quality of care in addition, this study will begin to identify a few of the most vital, areas that need improvement. QI teams will use this data for improving quality of care.

Defining a Quality of Care Framework

A quality of care framework for reproductive health services should be defined for the district. The elements of the quality framework and its indicators should be defined and shared with all the key stakeholders. This will help to demonstrate that the organization is firmly committed to quality improvement. The design team should visit various institutions and libraries to search available references for various quality of care framework and projects.

Training and Capacity Building for Quality Improvement

Training and capacity building for quality improvement for employees at all levels in the organization is absolutely essential and critical. Tom Peters suggests that creating a few good training programmes is not enough. We need to develop a continuous learning environment. After all, we are changing the culture, which is to say, we are changing attitudes. We do this by getting people to do things differently. This requires training, reinforcement, modelling, and more training – the creation and application of a continuous learning environment.

A central objective of the training activities is to develop skills in measuring, monitoring and improving quality as quickly as possible. In order to facilitate the programme's independence and self-determination, it is essential to develop local training capacity during the first year. All training activities will stress the importance of making a commitment to quality improvement through participation in quality training programmes and specific quality improvement projects. Thus participants will be of the importance of applying what they have learned from the outset.

Sensitization Workshops for State and District Officials

Quality improvement process is to be advertised internally and promoted just like any other major organization activity. Awareness and promotion should be handled in a relatively serious and businesslike manner, but with considerable enthusiasm and a demonstration of long-run commitment. The most effective way to promote quality improvement and to keep people aware of its benefits and potential is to utilise our most effective communication channels. Once quality improvement is understood and has taken hold, it will promote itself. Those employees who become involved with quality will become our most enthusiastic sales people, and the positive benefits of quality improvement will be readily apparent.

Health care quality as a concept has different facets, principles, techniques and tools. There is also a vast amount of literature written about it in the international media. Therefore, an early activity of the quality council is for its members to participate in a seminar on quality of care for reproductive health services. This seminar should be followed by intellectual discussions with the consultants as to the application of this concept in the district taking into consideration the available resources, the culture, and the current health status and structure. A similar activity should be organized to present quality of care to other key personnel in health care to get further support and to increase dissemination of the concept. These sessions, which should be attended by at least the quality coordinator and some members of the quality council, can serve as focus group sessions to get feedback on quality implementation and applications in health care as well as an avenue to increase awareness on the concept. Information and feedback collected from these sessions may be used in the next planning phase of implementation at the operational level and in launching experimental projects to raise awareness about the importance of improvement of quality among those who manage and deliver reproductive health services, and to develop local capacity to apply quality assurance methods in the district.

After this initial seminar, the central team will take on increasing responsibility for delivering the course and modifying its contents to make it more appropriate to the local context. They will begin to develop standardized training modules for the basic quality assurance course. The role of the international consultants increasingly became one of collegial support and feedback rather than one of teaching and leadership. As a result, this new programme's central team has strong leadership and technical capability.

Training Workshops for District level Officials and Medical Officers

The training workshops will be participated in by chief medical and health officer, deputy chief medical and health officer (CMHO), maternal and child health. officer, and other programme managers working at the district level. Apart from these, the junior specialists, senior medical officers, and medical officers working at the community health centres, block primary health centres and primary health centres will participate. The basic objective is to acquaint the participants with the project, the concept of quality of care, cost of poor quality, quality improvement process, quality cycle, and tools and techniques of measuring and improving quality of health care. It will help in creating an enabling environment in the district for improving quality of care. The estimated number of participants will be 175. A batch of 25 participants will be organized at a time. Therefore, in all 7 batches will be organized.

Quality Leadership Training

The leadership training for quality improvement will be imparted to quality improvement team leaders. The participants will include district level officers, and medical officer in-charge of community health centres and primary health centres. The participants will be trained in how to become effective leaders and supervisors for improving quality of care. After attending this course, the participants will be able to enhance their leadership qualities, which will facilitate the quality improvement processes in the district.

Training of Trainers for Quality Improvement

The district and block (community health centre/primary health centre) level officials will be first trained as trainers. The district medical and health services will organise a 5 day training of trainers on quality of care for reproductive health services. The participants of training of trainer's sessions would be state level officials, district level officials, and primary health centre medical officers. The purpose of providing the training of trainers is to allow the district level officials and medical officers to get acquainted with the various aspects of the quality of care. The participants once trained will go back to their respective health facilities.

Counselling Skill Training for Nursing Staff

A three-day course in interpersonal communication and counselling skills are to be organized for all the auxiliary nurse midwives and lady health visitors in the district. Basic theoretical information on communication and media will be incorporated into the training sessions, as well as practical steps and exercises. Participatory activities, small and whole group discussions, role playing will be the primary means of imparting skills. During the role-play, the trainees will have ample opportunity to assume the roles spouses, family members, clients, and counsellors. These training programmes will be organized at block primary health centre/community health centre level in the district. About 30 participants will attend each batch of the training programme. It is assumed that the block primary health centre/community health centre in-charge will make the necessary arrangements in the institution building for the training programme. Trainers would be selected from the identified trainers (Those who attended training of trainers and willing to become trainers for auxiliary nurse midwives/lady health visitors training). A team of four trainers would conduct this training programme. Among these four one trainer should be a lady doctor. The major responsibility of organizing these training programmes would be on deputy chief medical and health officer (family welfare).

Technical Competence Tainting for Nursing Staff

A three-day course in technical skills will be organized for all the auxiliary nurse midwives and lady health visitors in the district. Basic theoretical information on technical aspects of family planning methods and safe motherhood practices will be incorporated into the training sessions. Participatory activities, small and whole group discussions, role playing will be the primary means of imparting skills. During the role play, the trainees will have ample opportunity to assume the roles of spouses, family members, clients, and counsellors. These training programmes will be organized at block primary health centre/community health level in the district. About 30 participants will attend each batch of the training programme. It is assumed that the block primary health centre/community health centre in-charge will make the necessary arrangements in the institution building for the training programme. Trainers would be selected from the identified trainers (Those who attended training of trainers and willing to become trainers for auxiliary nurse midwives/lady health visitors training). A team of four trainers would conduct this training programme. Among these four, one trainer should be a lady doctor. The major responsibility of organizing these training programmes would be on deputy chief medical and health officer (family welfare).

Orientation Training for Private Medical Practitioners

The orientation training for programmes for all the private medical practitioners working in the district will be organized at district level. The participants will be acquainted with the project objectives, their role in improving the quality of reproductive health services, co-ordination with health department to provide quality services.

Refresher Training for Medical and Nursing Staff

A two-day refresher-training programme for medical and nursing staff will be conducted in the district during the second year of the project. The programme will be aimed to refresh the participants on quality of care principles and techniques and their applications for quality improvements.

Establishing Dual Record System

Home-based maternal records have proven their advantages in many ways (WHO, 1994). They get lost less frequently and move with the mother when she does, so that they are again available for the next interaction with the health system, whether it be another pregnancy, a family planning inquiry or treatment for a sexually transmitted diseases or anaemia. This record will cover three pregnancies or seven years, a more complete and integrated view of that women's reproductive health is maintained. Cards will be action-oriented and have the additional value of providing guidance to anyone who reads the cards as to what advice should be given to the woman for her delivery. The client-based records will be maintained at two levels: (a) at service provider's level; and (b) at service receiver's level. The card will be changed in case of lost. A new card could be issued on payment basis.

With a view to improving the quality of services a client-centred approach in recordkeeping should be introduced. The system of recording different services in different registers has been found to hinder this approach. This is so because the auxiliary nurse midwife does not have in front of her, a full record of the client's reproductive health needs when she meets her at home or in the sub-centre. If the auxiliary nurse midwife could have such a record, presumably she will be able to provide services in a comprehensive manner. Incidentally, if the clients can read their records, they themselves will know what services they are entitled to get. This card can be called *Family Reproductive Health Card*. It will improve the quality of supervision.

Potential Benefits of Dual Record System

This dual record system will have various potential benefits to clients, nursing staff (ANM/LHV), and facility managers (medical officer in-charge) working at primary health centres. The potential benefits are described below.

Potential Benefits to Clients: The potential benefits of dual record system to clients and their family are as follows:

- Encouraging continuity of care during pregnancy, labour, and the post-partum and inter-pregnancy periods.
- Promoting self-detection of risks and initiation of timely action.
- Promoting timely visit to referral centres.
- Serving as passport to care at health centres
- Fostering confidence in health workers and supervisors
- Encouraging family and community participation
- Providing a readily accessible record within the family

Potential Benefits to Health Workers: The potential benefits of dual record system to health workers and supervisors are as follows:

- Improving accountability to the client
- Improving monitoring of the progress and outcome of the services
- Improving client-worker interaction and relationship
- Helping to strengthen links among health workers
- Helping to improve the follow-up/continuity of services.
- Improving work planning and supervision

Potential Benefits to Managers: The potential benefits of dual record system to managers (medical officer in-charge) at the primary health centre are as follows:

- Strengthening the referral system
- Improving the quality of services

- Helping to involve the communities and their resources in health care
- Providing data to help measure actual output and desired output
- Improving accountability to the community of health care personnel

Designing the Dual Record System

It is suggested to change over to the dual-record system on a pilot basis in one primary health centre (PHC) during the second year of the project. A workshop will be organized for designing and institutionalizing the dual record system in the district. This workshop will be focused on important implementation issues such as card's functions, content, design, and production. For designing the cards, the following actions should be avoided:

- Do not include so much information that the card looks cluttered and confusing
- Do not design records containing written material alone for use
- Do not use colours or languages that are alien to the local culture of the district.
- Do not include subject matter that requires much writing
- Do not print large quantities of records before pre-testing the format.

It is suggested that this format be used as an instrument to be used in the mid-term and end-line evaluation by an independent agency. It will help in assessing the extent to which the health workers maintain client-based information and quality of services.

If possible, in areas where dual-record system is introduced, all eligible women in the community who may become pregnant should have cards, irrespective of whether or not they are currently pregnant or participating in family planning. The card should be issued during the first contact at home or in the sub-centre or primary health centre, and filled in regularly.

Initially, the cost of printing the cards will be borne by the project. However, 50 per cent of the printing costs will be recovered by instituting user fees. If the client demands a new card, in that case 100 per cent printing cost will be recovered from the client, so that the client will feel the importance of keeping the card safely.

Establishing Public Performance Rating System

The public performance rating will help and improve the behaviour of the team members for achieving the desired output. Rating will improve efficiency, performance, and reduce falsification. Rating should be with emotional impact. A workshop will be organized to frame the rating system for quality services at service unit level (team level), and to design key quality indicators and guidelines for the worker.

Public performance rating should be objective. When risk and rewards are decided on the basis of clear criteria, when they are developed by a team and managed by a group of persons, they become more objective. Experts are involved in such decision making. The leader gives up his role of deciding about risk and rewards, and passes this responsibility on to a team.

Rating is high leverage. It is suggested that at this stage, the ANMs at sub-centre level will not be rated for their performance. It is suggested to rate only facilities. In this case, we would introduce the rating system from the lower level institution (i.e., sub-centre level). The rating should not involve new data.

Rating should be done by an independent agency. The rating will cover all aspects of the adopted quality of care framework. Before publicly announcement, it should be shared with the quality teams and lead teams. The rating should be linked with a feasible risk and reward system. The rating system should be timely, transparent, easy to apply, easy to understand, objective in orientation, and be useful to improve the performance of the health worker in providing quality services. It should not be very rigid.

For the first round of quality assessment, the rating will not be publicly displayed, but a grace period will be provided to improve the performance. Later, it will be displayed at the sub-centre. The rating will be displayed at the sub-centre to make the community aware about the quality of services being provided by the respective sub-centre. The worker would like to be recognized in the community and among peers. So, it will force her to improve the quality of services to achieve the desired output. For this, a black board will be used to write the rating for the service quality being provided by the sub-centre. Information should be aggregate.

For example, a particular sub-centre may get a rating on service quality as "excellent", "average", or "poor". A detailed report on the rating should be posted to the sub-centre so that they can improve themselves on poor performing indicators. The objective of this rating system is to achieve high performance. So, it will definitely be linked to the risk and reward system. The consistently high performance service units should be identified to celebrate the quality on an annual "Quality Day" to be organized in the district, in which the Quality Council members should be present. The names of the high performance teams should be published by the organization. It will create a sense of responsibility in providing quality services. The district quality team should also release a press note in local newspapers about the high performers. It will show the concern and commitment of top level management in providing quality services. For recognizing and celebrating quality, some funds must be available with the district quality team.

Behaviour Change in Key Processors

At the level of individual manager, supervisor and employees successful strategy implementation often requires durable changes in personal behaviour. These changes typically require each individual to replace familiar, well-established activities with modified or new ones. Often, new skills must be learned. The impetus for such changes in behaviour is altered priorities and the need to develop and sustain focus on a few key issues and tasks. Table 6.4 shows the proposed behaviour change in the key processors of the system.

Table 6.4

Proposed Behaviour Change in the Key Processors of the System

Processor	*Present Situation*	*Proposed Change*
District level officers	Problem solving and decision-making done by senior managers and specialists	Problem solving and decision-making will be done in collaboration with staff and based on hard data
	Do not discuss quality of care in the monthly meetings of medical officer in-charge of block PHCs. They discusses about targets and achievements only	Quality of care will be discussed in meetings at every level
	Monitoring is being done by field visits to health centres, but it is irregular and not focused on quality of care	Should visit SC/PHC as per plan regularly and during their visit they should discuss the issues of quality of care
	Quality costs money	Quality saves money
	Authority is awarded	Capabilities will be rewarded
Medical officer	Short-term improvements made, often at point of crisis (reactive)	Gradual, continuous improvements made in all functions (Proactive)
	Control and direct staff	Encourage the staff to take initiative
	Do not respect the contribution of staff	Contribution by staff will be respected
	Not provide supportive supervision to nursing staff	Provide supportive supervision and encourage to take initiative
	Do not analyse data for root cause	Root cause analysis will be done to see the problem

Cont'd ...

Cont'd ...

	Decisions about process improvements are not based on facts	Service statistics data will be analysed to suggest possible solutions. Medical officer in-charge will use the data to determine the nature and size of the problems, and to justify any decisions made to improve process
	Do not use different quality tools to plan, do, study and act	Use of quality improvement tools such as brainstorming, affinity diagram, cause-and-effect diagram, flow chart for improving quality
ANM	Do not focus client-centred approach	Focus on client-centred approach
	Family planning method are not provided on informed choices	Family planning methods will be provided on informed choices
	Information imparted during service contact are not complete to enable clients to choose and employ	Complete information will be to clients about the methods and services
	Clients are not treated with respect	Clients will be treated with respect
	Not spending ample time with each client	Ample time will be spent with each client
	Clients are not encouraged to ask questions	Clients will be encouraged to ask questions
	Irregular follow-up visits to clients	Ensure at least three antenatal care visits and two postnatal care visits and for family planning clients mechanism to maintain continuity will improve

Strategic Control

Strategic control is an important part of the strategic management process. It may be applied at any level in the organization, even at the district level in our example. Strategic control provides top management a means of determining whether the organization is performing satisfactorily and an explicit process for refining or completely altering the strategy. Strategic control involves agreeing upon objectives, measuring and evaluating performance against the objectives, and taking corrective action, if necessary. More specifically, control is defined as a combination of components that act together to ensure that the level of actual output comes as close as possible to a set of desired output.

A strategic control system is a system to support health managers in assessing how well the quality improvement strategy compares to its progress in the accomplishment of its goals and, when discrepancies are detected, to support areas that need attention. Therefore, the strategic control system monitors, evaluates, and adjusts the strategic implementation, the strategy itself, and the situational analysis processes. The strategic control system, as it monitors the progress, should provide early warning signals that something may be wrong. If the district is not making progress toward improving the quality of care by achieving its objectives, the strategic control process will call for additional investigation. This process may reveal the faulty reasoning of the past or the new environmental conditions that impair the strategy.

The control system will provide a method for health managers to evaluate the strategy and initiate required changes. By monitoring performance and identifying deviations from agreed upon objectives, the strategic control system provides the signals that trigger management intervention in the selection, adjustment, or implementation of the strategy. The strategic control system will be able to periodically measure progress, make comparisons to the objectives, determine the problems, and take corrective action for improving quality of care in the district.

In order to be effective, it is important that controls have certain characteristics. For controls to be effective, they should: be based on accurate, relevant, and timely information; be directed at controlling only the critical elements; be flexible; be cost-effective; be simple and easy to understand; be timely; and emphasize the exceptions (Duncan et al., 1995). The proposed control mechanism will be directed at only a few critical elements to achieve the desired performance. Control systems will be both flexible and cost-effective, so as it will be easy to implement. Controls system will not determine decisions; rather, health managers should be allowed to make decisions within acceptable boundaries.

The proposed control system will be simple and easy to understand. Controls that are overly complex or difficult to apply will be ignored or applied incorrectly. Therefore, management will work to keep controls simple.

Keeping the above-mentioned characteristics of a good strategic control system, a multi-tiered control process will be designed in the district. It will consist of three modes: monthly review, quarterly report, and an annual review. The monthly review will be used to identify obstacles to progress towards achieving the desired output, encourage timely corrective action, and document lessons learned. The quarterly review will be used to channel local lessons upward, integrate organization-wide efforts, modify the implementation themes, and understand key obstacles to progress. The annual reviews will be used to study the results, evaluate and improve the planning process, identify issues for the next planning cycle, and modify the planning cycle.

References

Askew, Ian, Barbara Mensch and Alfred Adewuyi (1994). "Indicators for Measuring the Quality of Family Planning Services in Nigeria". *Studies in Family Planning,* Volume 25, Number 5: 268–83.

AVSC (Association for Voluntary Surgical Contraception) (1994). *COPE: Client Oriented, Provider Efficient Services: A Tool for Continuous Quality Improvement*. New York: AVSC, Unpublished.

Brown, Lisanne, Mostafa Tyane, Jane Bertrand, Don Lauro, Mohamed Abou-ouakil and Lisa deMaria (1995). "Quality of Care in Family Planning Services in Morocco". *Studies in Family Planning,* Volume 26, Number 3: 154–68.

Brown, Lori DiPrete, L. Franco, N. Rafeh and T. Hatzell (1993). "Quality Assurance of Health Care in Developing Countries". *Quality Assurance Methodology Refinement Series*, Bethesda: Quality Assurance Project.

Bruce, Judith (1983). *Users' Perspectives on Family Planning: Some Operational and Research Issues*. New York: The Population Council.

—— (1990). "Fundamental Elements of Quality of Care: A Simple Framework". *Studies in Family Planning,* Volume 21, Number 2: 61–91.

Calla, Cynthia (1991). "Translating Concepts of Total Quality Management to Improve Quality of Health Care in Family Planning Service Delivery Programmes in Developing Countries". A Briefing Paper presented for the Family Planning Service Division, Office of Population, USAID.

Center for Health Research, Consultation and Education (CIAES) and the Mother Care Project (1991). *Qualitative Research on Knowledge, Attitudes and Practices Related to Women's Reproductive Health.* Arlington, VA: Mother Care Project.

Crosby, P.B. (1982). *Quality is Free.* New York: McGraw Hill.

Deming, W.E. (1982). *Quality, Productivity and Competitive Position.* Cambridge, MA: Massachusetts Institute of Technology, Centre for Advanced Engineering Study.

Department of Family Welfare (Evaluation), Government of Rajasthan and Indian Institute of Health Management Research (1997). *Concurrent Evaluation of Reproductive Health and Child Care in Rajasthan: State Evaluation Report* (Cycle I, April-September, 1996), Jaipur: GoR/IIHMR.

Department of Family Welfare, Ministry of Health and Family Welfare, Government of India (1996). *Manual for Orientation of Auxiliary Nurse Midwives and Supervisor.* New Delhi: GoI.

Directorate of Census Operations Rajasthan (1994). *Census of India, 1991.* Series 21, Rajasthan, Part XII (A and B), District Census Handbook, District Udaipur, Jaipur: Office of the Joint Director, Census Operations Rajasthan.

Directorate of Medical, Health and Family Welfare Services, Government of Rajasthan (1995). Budget Documents of Medical, Health and Family Welfare Services (1991–95). Jaipur GoR.

Directorate of Medical, Health and Family Welfare Services, Government of Rajasthan (1996). Annual Progress Report of Medical, Health and Family Welfare Services (1995–96). Jaipur GoR.

Donabedian, Avedis (1980). *The Definition of Quality and Approaches to Its Management. Volume 1. Explorations in Quality Assessment and Monitoring.* Ann Arbor, Michigan: Health Administration Press.

Donabedian, Avedis (1988). "The Quality of Care: How can it be Assessed?" *Journal of the American Medical Association,* Volume 260, Number 12: 1743–48.

Duncan, W. Jack, Peter M. Ginter and Linda E. Swayne (1995). *Strategic Management of Health Care Organisations.* Cambridge, MA: Blackwell Publishers.

Fisher, Andrew, Barbara Mensch, Robert Miller, Ian Askew, Anrudh Jain, Cecelia Ndeti, Lewis Ndhlovu and P. Tapsoba (1992). *Guidelines and Instruments for a Family Planning Situation Analysis.* New York: The Population Council.

Geyndt, Willy De (1995). "Managing the Quality of Health Care in Developing Countries". World Bank Technical Paper No. 258, Washington, DC.

Government of India (1983). National Health Policy, 1983. New Delhi: Ministry of Health & Family Welfare.

Government of India (2002). National Health Policy, 2002. New Delhi: Ministry of Health & Family Welfare.

Government of India (2005). National Rural Health Mission, Meeting People's Health Needs in Rural Areas: Framework for Implementation 2005–*2012*. New Delhi: Ministry of Health & Family Welfare, Government of India.

Goyal, R.S., Ch. Satish Kumar and Sunita Nigam (1996). *A Demographic Profile of Districts in Rajasthan on the Basis of Eligible Couple Registers: District Udaipur*. Jaipur: IIHMR.

Gupta, S.D., K.M. Sathyanarayana, Jaimala Gupta, N.K. Sharma, Nutan P. Jain and P.R. Sodani (1996). Report of End-of-the Project Evaluation: Health & Family Welfare Area Project, Rajasthan (Phase II). Jaipur: IIHMR.

Haffey, Joan, Margot L. Zimmerman and Gordon W. Perkin (1984). "Communicating Contraception". *Populi*, Volume 11, Number 2.

Hardee, Karen (1994). "Client Perspectives, Needs and Wants". Partnerships, Opportunities and Challenges: A Vision for the Future. Paper presented at USAID Cooperating Agencies Meeting, Washington, DC.

Hardee, Karen and Brian Gould (1993). "A Process for Quality Improvement in Family Planning Services". *International Family Planning Perspectives*, Volume 19, Number 4: 147–52.

—— (1992). "A Process for Service Quality Improvement in Family Planning". Durham, NC: Family Health International.

Helzner, Judith (1990). Report of the Subcommittee on Quality Indicators in Family Planning Service Delivery. Report submitted to the USAID Task Force on Standardization of Family Planning programme Performance Indicators, Washington, DC: POPTECH.

Hudgins, A.A. and L. Merino (1988). "Computerized Patient Flow Analysis in Costa Rica". Paper presented at the Annual Meeting of the Population Association of America, New Orleans, Louisiana, April 21–23.

Huezo, Carlos and Soledad Diaz (1993). "Quality of Care in Family Planning: Clients' Rights and Providers' Needs". *Advances in Contraception*, Volume 9: 129–39.

International Institute for Population Sciences (IIPS) (1995). National Family Health Survey (MCH and Family Planning), India 1992–93. Bombay: IIPS.

Jain, Anrudh K. (1989). "Fertility Reduction and the Quality of Family Planning Services". *Studies in Family Planning*, Volume 20, Number 1: 1–16.

Jain, Anrudh K., Judith Bruce and Barbara Mensch (1992). "Setting Standards of Quality in Family Planning Programs". *Studies in Family Planning*, Volume 23, Number 6: 392–95.

Jain, Sagar C. (1988). "A Diagnostic Approach for the Improvement of Health Manpower Management". *Health Services Management Research*, Volume 1, Number 2, July: 101–11.

—— (1997). Personal Communication during the Course.

Katz, K., Karen Hardee and M. Villinski (1993). *Quality of Care in Family Planning: A Catalog of Assessment and Improvement Tools*. Durham, NC: Family Health International.

Kaufman, Joan, Zhang Zhirong, Qiao Xinjian and Zhang Yang (1992). "The Quality of Family Planning Service in Rural China". *Studies in Family Planning*, Volume 23, Number 2: 73–84.

Keller, Alan B. (1973). "Patient Attrition in Five Mexico City Family Planning Clinics", in J. Mayone Stycos (ed.), *Clinics, Contraception and Communication*. Des Moines: Meredith Corporation.

Kim, Young-Mi, Jose Rimon, Kim Winnard, Carol Corso, I.V. Mako, Sebioniga Lawal, Stella Babalola and Dale Huntington (1992). "Improving the Quality of Service Delivery in Nigeria". *Studies in Family Planning*, Volume 23, Number 2: 118–27.

Kumar, Sushil, Anrudh K. Jain and Judith Bruce (1989). "Assessing the Quality of Family Planning Services". Programs Division Working Paper No. 2, New York: The Population Council.

Lapham, Robert J. and B. Simmons (eds.) (1987). *Organizing for Effective Family Planning Programmes*. Washington, DC: The National Academy Press.

Lapham, Robert J. and W. Parker Mauldin (1985). "Contraceptive Prevalence: The Influence of Organised Family Planning Programs". *Studies in Family Planning*, Volume 16, Number 3: 117–30.

Leslie, Joanne and Geeta Rao Gupta (1989). *Utilisation of Formal Services for Maternal Nutrition and Health Care*. Washington, DC: International Center for Research on Women.

Lipton, Helene L., Ruth Dixon-Mueller and Philip R. Lee (1987). "Client-provider Transactions: An Introduction and Conceptual Overview", in Robert Lapham and George Simmons (eds.), *Organising for Effective Family Planning Programs*. Washington, DC: National Academy Press.

Locay, Luis, W. Sanderson and Ethel Carillo Weeks (1990). *Prenatal Care in Peru*. Washington, DC: International Center for Research on Women.

Loegering, Lisa, R. Reiter and J. Gambone (1994). "Measuring the Quality of Health Care". *Clinical Obstetrics and Gynecology*, Volume 37, Number 1: 122–36.

MacStravic, Robin E. Scott, Edward Mahn and Deborah C. Reedal (1983). "Portfolio Analysis for Hospital". *Health Care Management Review*, Fall.

Mensch, Barbara (1992). "Quality of Care: A Neglected Dimension", in Marjorie Koblinsky, J. Timyan and J. Gay (eds.), *The Health of Women: A Global Perspective*. Boulder, CO: Westview Press, pp. 235–53.

—— (1993). "Using Data on Client-provider Interactions to Assess the Quality of Family Planning Services: A Methodological Note". Paper presented at the Expert Meeting on Information Systems and Measurement for Assessing programme Effects, Committee on Population, National Academy of Sciences, Washington, DC, September 9–10.

—— (1994). "Using Situation Analysis to Develop Quality of Care Indicators: Examples from Ghana, Nigeria and Tanzania". Proceedings of the Africa OR/TA Project Conference, Nairobi, Kenya: The Population Council.

Mernissi, Fatima (1975). "Obstacles to Family Planning Practice in Urban Morocco". *Studies in Family Planning*, Volume 6, Number 12: 418–25.

Mundigo, Axel (1973). "Honduras Revisited: The Clinic and Its Clientele", in J. Mayone Stycos (ed.), *Clinics, Contraception and Communication: Evaluation Studies of Family Planning Programs in Four Latin American Countries*. New York: Appleton-Century-Crofts.

Novaes, Humberto de Moraes (1993). "The Implementation of Quality Assurance Programs through Hospital Accreditation in Latin America and the Caribbean". Paper prepared for FHI/PAHO Workshop, Quality of Care in Reproductive Health, Research Triangle Park, NC, March 25–27.

Pariani, Siti, David M. Heer and Maurice D. Van Arsdol, Jr. (1987). "Continued Contraceptive Use in Five Family Planning Clinics in Surabaya, Indonesia". Paper presented at the 115th Annual Meeting of the American Public Health Association, New Orleans, Louisiana, October 19–22.

—— (1991). "Does Choice Make a Difference to Contraceptive Use: Evidence from East Java". *Studies in Family Planning*, Volume 22, Number 6: 384–90.

Parker, Laurie, Geeta Rao Gupta, Kathleen Kurz and Kathleen Merchant (1990). *Better Health for Women: Research Results from the Maternal Health Care Program*. Washington, DC: International Center for Research on Women.

Pathfinder International (1993). *Family Planning Quality of Care in Asia*. Bangladesh: Centre for Development Management.

Pebley, Ann R. and James W. Brackett (1982). "The Relationship of Contraceptive Availability to Contraceptive Use". *International Family Planning Perspectives*, Volume 8, Number 3: 84–92.

Phillips, James F., Ruth Simmons, Marjorie A. Koenig and Mian Bazle Hossian (1986). "Worker Client Exchanges and the Dynamics of Contraceptive Use in Rural Bangladesh". Paper presented at the Annual Meeting of the Population Association of America, San Francisco, April 3–5.

Planning Department (1993). *Eighth Five-Year Plan (1992–97)*. Jaipur: Planning Department, Government of Rajasthan.

Potter, Joseph E., Octavio Mojarro and Leopoldo Nunez (1987). "The Influence of Maternal Health Care on Contraceptive Acceptance in Rural Mexico". *Studies in Family Planning*, Volume 18, Number 3: 144–56.

Prabhavathi, K. and A. Shenshadri (1987). "Pattern of IUD Use: Follow-up of Acceptors in Mysore". *Journal of Family Welfare*, Volume 35, Number 1: 3–16.

Racoveanu, N. and K.S. Johansen (1995). "Technology for the Continuous Improvement of the Quality of Health Care". *World Health Forum*, Volume 16: 128–44.

Rahman, Makhlislur, W.H. Mosley, Atiqur Rahman Khan, A.I. Chowdhury and J. Chakraborty (1990). "Contraceptive Distribution in Bangladesh: Some Lessons Learned". *Studies in Family Planning*, Volume 11, Number 6: 191–212.

Roberts, D., P. Panitchpakdi and B. Loevinsohn (1993). "Reducing Discontinuation in Family Planning Programs". *The Family Planning Manager*, Volume 2, Number 3.

Rogow, Debbie (1986). "Quality of Care in International Family Planning: A Feminist Contribution", in *The Contraceptive Development Process and Quality of Care in Reproductive Health Services*. New York: International Women's Health Coalition and The Population Council.

Rowe, Alan J., Richard O. Mason, Karl E. Dickel and Neil H. Snyder (1989). *Strategic Management: A Methodological Approach*. 3rd ed. Reading, Massachusetts: Addison-Wesley Publishing Company.

Satia, Jay (1994). "Improving Quality of Care in Population Programmes", in *Innovative Approaches to Population Programmes Management-Quality of Care*. Malaysia: ICOMP, Volume 1.

—— (1993). *Improving Quality of Care in Population Programmes*. Malaysia: ICOMP, October.

Scrimshaw, Susan (1976). "Women's Modesty: One Barrier to the Use of Family Planning Clinics in Ecuador", in John F. Marshall and Steven Polgar (eds.), *Culture, Natality and Family Planning*. Chapel Hill: University of North Carolina Press.

Simmons, George B. and Robert J. Lapham (1987). "The Effectiveness of Family Planning Programs", in Robert Lapham and George Simmons (eds.), *Organising for Effective Family Planning Programs*. Washington, DC: National Academy Press.

Simmons, Ruth and George Simmons (1992). "Moving towards a Higher Quality of Care: Challenges for Management", in Anrudh K. Jain (ed.), *Managing Quality of Care in Population Programs*. West Hartford, CT: Kumarian Press.

Simmons, Ruth and James F. Phillips (1990). "The Proximate Operational Determinants of Fertility Regulation Behaviour". Research Division Working Paper No. 15, NY: The Population Council.

Simmons, Ruth and Christopher Elias (1994). "The Study of Client-provider Interactions: A Review of Methodological Issues". *Studies in Family Planning*, Volume 25, Number 1: 1–17.

Simmons, Ruth, M.A. Koblinsky and James F. Phillips (1985). "Client Relations in South Asia: Their Programmatic and Societal Determinants". Paper presented at IUSSP Conference, Jamaica, April 10–13.

Snowden, Robert (1972). "Social and Personal Factors involved in the Use-effectiveness of the IUD", in Robert Snowden and Alfredo Goldsmith (eds.), *Family Planning Research Conference: A Multidisciplinary Approach* (Proceedings). Amsterdam: Excerpta Medica.

Srinivasan, Venkatesh (1996). "Improving Quality of Family Welfare Services in Bundi District". A Paper submitted to the UNC-CH in Partial Fulfillment of the Requirement for the Degree of MPH in the Department of Health Policy and Administration, Chapel Hill.

Thaddeus, Sereen and Deborah Maine (1990). *Too Far to Walk: Maternal Mortality in Context*. New York: Centre for Population and Family Health, School of Public Health, Faculty of Medicine, Columbia University.

Tinker, Ann, M. Koblinsky, P. Daly, C. Rooney, C. Leighton, M. Griffiths, Z. Huque and Barbara Kwast (1993). *Making Motherhood Safe*. Washington, DC: World Bank.

UNFPA (1992). Family Welfare Area Project (Himachal Pradesh, Rajasthan and Maharashtra) Mid-term Review, Final Reports. New Delhi: UNFPA.

Van der Waal, M.A., A.F. Casparie and C.J. Lako (1996). "Quality of Care: A Comparison of Preferences between Medical Specialists and Patients with Chronic Diseases". *Social Science and Medicine*, Volume 4, Number 2: 643–49.

Veney, James, Robert Magnani and Famina Gorbach (1993). "Measurement of the Quality of Family Planning Services". *Population Research and Policy Review*, Volume 12: 243–59.

Wedderburn, Maxine and Mona Moore (1990). *Qualitative Assessment of Attitudes Affecting Childbirth Choices of Jamaican Women*. Arlington, VA: Mother Care.

Whelan, Elizabeth (1974). "Compliance with Contraceptive Regimes". *Studies in Family Planning*, Volume 5, Number 11: 349–55.

WHO (1994). Home-Based Records: Guidelines for Development, Adaption and Evaluation. Geneva: WHO.

Word Bank (1995). Policy and Finance Strategies for Strengthening Primary Health Care Services. Report Number 13042-IN, South Asia Country Department II (India), Population and Human Resources Division, Washington, DC.

Index